Two Farms
Essays on a Maine Country Life

Janet Galle

ILLUSTRATIONS BY
Arek W. Galle

© 2004 Janet Galle
All Rights Reserved. No part of this publication may be reproduced or transmitted in any form or by any means, electronic or mechanical, including photocopy, recording or any other information storage and retrieval system, without prior permission in writing from Janet Galle.

PUBLISHED BY
Galle Farm

WEBSITE
www.gallefarm.com

DESIGNED BY
Will-Dale Press

COVER DESIGN
Leonard Commet Krill
Horizon Graphic Services

COVER PHOTO
A. Jacob Galle

ILLUSTRATIONS
Arek W. Galle

PRINTED BY
Will-Dale Press
Bowdoin, Maine

ISBN
0-9663663-3-6

To my family and Cassie

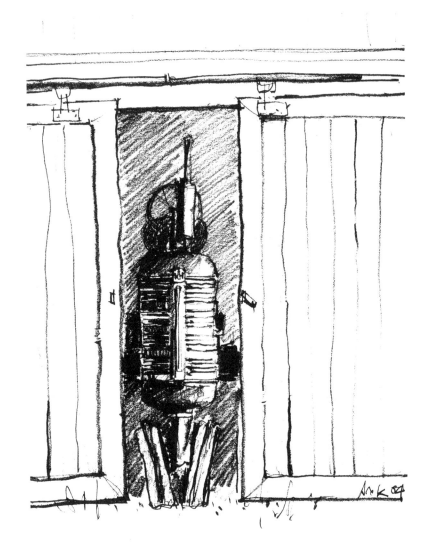

Contents

ACKNOWLEDGMENTS   VIII
PROLOGUE

A SALTWATER FARM
BOOK I: AN OCEAN VIEW   1
Crickets, October, 1981   1
The Shepherd, December, 1981   2
Quills, February, 1982   3
Robin Snow, April, 1982   4
Tastes Like Salt Water, August, 1982   5
A Blackberry End to Summer, September, 1982   6
Piggy Pork, October, 1982   8
Twins, December, 1982   9
Midwinter on Ice, February, 1983   10
Skunk! March, 1983   11
Greta's Death, April, 1983   13
Pink Tea, June, 1983   14
Tractor Dreams, September, 1983   15
Sweet Harvest, October, 1983   17
Primary Form, November, 1983   18
Six Geese A-laying, December, 1983   19
Out Like a Lamb, March, 1984   21
SWAT Team, July, 1984   23
Hideaways, August, 1984   24
Ghost Fog, October, 1984   26
The Cycle of Things, November, 1984   27
Hunger Moon, February, 1985   29
Gentle Richard, April, 1985   30
Before Color was Invented, May, 1985   32
Raiders, Again, July, 1985   33

APPLE CREEK FARM

BOOK II: 130 ACRES 36
Halfway Around the World, November, 1985 36
"Wake me," December, 1985 38
The Art of Seed Selection, February, 1986 39
Spring Fever, April, 1986 40
Pshaw, June, 1986 42
Got That Summer Feeling, July, 1986 43
A Single Tree, September, 1986 45
Hatchet Day, November, 1986 47
Strap on the Skis, January, 1987 49
Fling Open a Window, May, 1987 50
Windmills, June, 1987 52
Groundhogs and Mothers, July, 1987 54
Frog Patrol, August, 1987 56
A Mouthful of Air, November, 1987 58
The Heritage of Lambs, April, 1988 59
Neighbors, June, 1988 61
Flashdance in the Barn, October, 1988 63
Land, January, 1989 64

BOOK III: VISITORS 67
30,000 Cubic Miles, March, 1989 67
Baseball for Women, June, 1989 69
Tomorrow It Might Be Spring, March, 1990 71
Cat's Eye View, August, 1990 72
A Routine Miracle, December, 1990 74
Celebrate As One, July, 1991 76
Lucky Kitten, August, 1991 78
Making Hay, September, 1991 81
A Motherless Lamb, January, 1992 83
Squirrels Always Win, February, 1992 85
Ravens, April, 1992 87

Forest Intrigue, October, 1992	88
Circus Mice, November, 1992	91
Escape to the Barn, December, 1992	92
Contented and Nowhere Else To Be, July, 1993	94
Blue, August, 1993	96
Garden Visitors, September, 1993	98
Dogs Go to Town, February, 1994	100
A Touch of Grace, May, 1994	102
On Skunks and Chickens, November, 1994	103

BOOK IV: TRUTHS — 106

Celebrate Winter with a Walk, December, 1994	106
Spring Signs, March, 1995	108
Birding with a Friend, May, 1995	110
A Groundhog Truce, June, 1995	111
Loss, October, 1995	113
Gone Unnoticed, December, 1995	115
Titans of the Forest, January, 1996	116
Life Seen from a New Angle, March, 1996	118
Nell, April, 1996	120
I Know Where the Red Trillium Grow, May, 1996	122
The Moon Plays Games, October, 1996	123
Huck Comes Out of Hibernation, February, 1997	125
A City Cat Comes to Stay, June, 1997	127
I Hate the Tractor, September, 1997	128
Mushrooms, Bats, and Poe, October, 1997	130
A Red Ribbon, November, 1997	132
Stan and Monty, Two Old Men, December, 1997	134
The Trees are Still Standing, January, 1998	135

POSTSCRIPT: That Which is Seen, October, 2004	139
EPILOGUE	143

Acknowledgments

In gathering this collection I owe much to many people. First and most important are the members of my family. My children, especially Jillian, demanded that I finally find the time to write and collect these essays. Her thoughtful advice has clarified the wording of the acknowledgments and postscript. Arek spent hours with me, guiding the style of the book itself and providing all the drawings. Jacob organized the photography, patiently scanned photos, and instructed me in computer use. My husband Pete has always encouraged me. He is the real farmer in our family (having grown up on a truck farm in Ohio) and the one who has put up with all my projects and crazy ideas. He also shovels all the garden manure, takes care of the sheep (and now our cow) on a daily basis, and looks out for me.

John Cole, who was my neighbor in Brunswick, had often encouraged me to publish my writing. ("You should sell your columns 17 times over," he once told me.) I never thought much about "selling" my columns, but I have wanted to bring something dear to my heart to fruition.

Clare Howell of Old Books in Brunswick, Maine, was the final catalyst that made this book actually come into print. On June 23, 2004 at the screening of one of Jacob's films, she asked me when I was going to gather my essays into a book. I hedged. On June 25 she gave me Dale Woerter's card and urged me to do it. Dale Woerter and KymNoelle Sposato at Will-Dale Press in Bowdoin provided the structure for this collection in a wonderful, summer brainstorming session.

Without Lucretia McDine, my first editor at the *The Times Record*, there would have been no "Country Ways." She looked at my first submission and gave me a chance. The title of my column was her creation. She wrote the back of this book, as well. Virginia Wright and Barbara Bartels supported me as editors at *The Times Record*. Without the commitment of these three women to a quiet column about rural life, my writing would not have continued.

Over the years the readers of "Country Ways" sent letters of appreciation which encouraged me. I often feel like I am in isolation when I write, and their feedback was important, as was the support of the writing group who met regularly for years at Jane Lamb's. Two years ago Nancy Heiser loaned me a book about publishing. She doesn't know how much that helped.

Jeff Fischer, my colleague at Mt. Ararat High School in Topsham, Maine where I teach English, has dedicated hours to the most careful copy editing of this manuscript. Jeff is a superb writer, and his fine eye caught so much that escaped my view. Any errors that remain are all mine.

Leonard Krill, with whom I team taught journalism for nine years, is a master of web design and owner of Horizon Graphic Services — and the one I turn to for advice on a daily basis. I am a better teacher and thinker because of his influence. He organized my web site and designed the cover of this book using Jacob's photography. Sheila Bohlin, art teacher at Mt. Ararat, showed me how to scan Jacob's slides.

Sue Chadima has been our faithful vet. Ray Youmans has helped with the big ram, and Russ Pinfold cared for our oldest ewe Cassie. We have bought grain, chickens, tractor parts, and supplies — and received advice and support — from a multitude of agricultural sources, commercial ones like Raymond Knight in Richmond, Anita Delecto in Auburn, Gary Brooks in Brunswick, and Jesse Harriman in Richmond, and our fellow farmers — Richard Morin, George Christopher, Tom Settlemire, Brant Miller, the Woods family, the Biettes, Bart and Karen Barstis, Lee Straw, the Hydes, and Bill and Rosie Guest.

My father Chester William Schmidt, who died in 1995, and my mother Doris Alta Youngen Schmidt, who still visits Maine every summer, provided me with a grounded upbringing in rural Indiana, which included many trips across the United States and frequent visits to both sets of grandparents in Ohio and Pennsylvania. Without these experiences, my curiosity about the natural world would not have developed. I love my parents dearly for all they have given me.

My family, my brothers Jack and Jim and sister Jill, my nieces and nephews, friends, neighbors, and animals who appear in these stories are ultimately the reason that any of this was written. They provide testimony to the passing of days and greatly enrich the view from a farm life.

Prologue

When I was ten years old, my father took a movie of me pretending to be a writer. I was sitting at a card table, shuffling papers and writing with a pencil. Pop caught that picture, a clear image, through the dining room window. Fifty years later the film is faded. My interest in recording episodes and events, however, never vanished, although for many years I did other things — married, moved from Indiana to Maine, raised three children, taught school, learned about birds, worked in my garden and on our small farm — an ordinary life.

Then in November, 1979, as editor of the Merrymeeting Audubon Society's newsletter, I began writing about our farm life and our family's interactions with the natural world. In September, 1981, I wrote my first column, "Country Ways," for the *The Times Record*, a daily midcoast community newspaper. That single column turned into 200 more, which were published every month or so from 1981 to 1998. The essays in this collection *Two Farms*, which have not been altered from their original intent, are drawn from that body of writing.

My husband Pete grew up on a truck farm near Dayton, Ohio. I grew up in the middle of soybean fields in eastern Indiana. After college at Miami University, we began farming in Maine when we moved to four acres on the edge of Middle Bay, part of Casco Bay, in 1968. All three of our children, Arek, Jillian, and Jacob, were born there. Many of our animals whose lives are reflected in these essays began their days on that small saltwater farm. Pete built the barn, and although it was not big, it was large enough for a rural existence. We learned how to grow our own vegetables, and the children learned about life and death.

In 1985 we moved inland, to a forest which had once been a farm. The land where we now live is crisscrossed with stone walls, testimonies to the hard labor of farmers who went before us. We call this place Apple Creek Farm. A small stream runs on the north and west of our house and the last of the old orchard, three trees, blooms on the east side. Deep in the woods we still find productive apple trees. We have a pond now to replace our ocean view and much more land which we hay. We harvest timber from the extensive forests. Ultimately, however, the direction that all of our lives have taken is the real product of living on two farms. Those stories are told in this collection of essays.

Book I: An Ocean View

Crickets
October, 1981

Nose to nose, the cricket on one side encountered the towhead on the other. This wonderful, hopping, singing creature had deserted the safety of the meadow to scamper about on the gravel road as if his sole purpose in life was to entertain my young son.

Hand in hand, Jacob and I had ventured forth on a cricket hunt, a simple task in an October meadow. The earth basked in the autumn sunshine, as it streamed through red and golden leaves. Behind us, the deep green waters of the bay stretched toward islands where no one lived. The day seemed suspended in time with no place to go, no job to be done, and only crickets on our minds. We found them everywhere, at our feet.

Under the dying meadow grasses, tiny black wonders of the insect world scrambled about and then disappeared — all but this one brave cricket — who had jumped onto a country road to delight a small boy.

We walked on, passing the side-delivery hay rake standing idle after its summer work. Jacob pulled a crisp McIntosh from his jacket pocket. We shared bites.

Ahead of us stood a fading milkweed patch, and our hunt changed from crickets to caterpillars. We found a monarch, his warning colors of black, yellow, and white standing in sharp contrast to the dull green of the milkweed leaf. Unlike the crickets, this caterpillar commanded us to be quiet. With voracious appetite, he ate, black horns wagging, as he prepared for the stillness and peace of the chrysalis.

We clasped hands again and quickened our pace; the air was getting cooler; the sun was setting. Down the road near our red mailbox a sudden movement on the ground caught Jacob's eye, and we approached cautiously. A flicker, marked with intricate brown feathers that hid a surprise of yellow underneath, hopped to a depression in the road which retained the clear water from last night's rainfall. He drank quickly, tilting his head upward, then paused to look directly at us. We held our breath. We were inches away.

The flicker moved back again to the grassy roadside where he beat at the ants buried among the weed roots. The red marking on his head moved up and down rapidly as he fed at dusk. Tomorrow this flicker would continue his southward migration and leave us behind.

It is evening now, and my son sleeps. From my porch I watch the maple tree, cloaked in brilliant orange, one by one dropping its life-sustaining leaves. There is no breeze, and the leaves fall quietly, gently, to rest at the tree's base. There they nestle among the crinkled, fading mahogany carpet which will slowly return to the earth. The air is crisp, like my son's apple, and I go inside for a wool sweater.

The Shepherd
December, 1981

Each evening, after all traces of red have left the sky and the trees no longer stand etched on the western horizon, I head toward the barn. As I walk the frozen pathway, I stop and look above me. Watching the sky in December is like looking through a precisely focused telescope. Every star is distinct. Even distant pinpoints of sparkle seem defined, exact, and close. The Big Dipper rests almost on the treetops which border the northern edge of the meadow. Orion's belt gleams in the east. The vast galaxy above me twinkles with the sparkling sense of anticipation this month carries.

The barn, too, is filled with anticipation, and I like to spend quiet moments captured by its animal warmth. Seven ewes stand at the barn's eastern door waiting patiently to be let inside. Cold may bother me, but it does not bother my sheep. I swing the gate open, and they come in quickly, in the ritualistic order that they follow every single night. Cassie first, Shamrock last, and five in-between.

I have filled the manger with sweet-smelling hay, reminiscent of a hot July afternoon. Grain is in the feeder. The smell of their molasses-laced feed is like the holiday kitchen smell of cookies baking. Their bucket overflows with icy water, freshly drawn.

The sheep line either side of the manger to eat, as I walk between them, scratching ears, talking quietly of the events to come. I check Cassie carefully, her sides bulging with what I hope will be healthy twins. She is my oldest and favorite ewe and will have her seventh lambing in January in this barn, a haven from the blowing snows and bitter winds. For the sheep, December is a comfortable month, snug and quiet in a barn that provides the security for their lambs to be born in midwinter. My husband built this barn for these sheep as a protection against nature's vagaries. Now those sheep give to us in return — wool and food and miracles such as lambs.

My chores are done, but in December I can never leave the barn quickly. I shove my hands deeper into my pockets, stomp my cold feet, and watch my breath make clouds in the frosty air. When the ewes have finished eating, they will settle down to chew their cuds contentedly. A bit of that contentment rubs off on me, reminding me of the spirit that dwells within a barn, a spirit I wish to keep amidst the holiday bustle.

There is a wonderfully warm wood stove waiting in the house, but first, one last word from the tending shepherd. Then the light is extinguished, the door closed and bolted. There is a legend that promises that barn animals will speak on Christmas Eve. Perhaps, but even if it is only a tale, a barn still seems the appropriate place to tarry a while in December.

Quills
February, 1982

Life in the country produces inevitable confrontations with wild critters. By hook or by crook, these clever creatures of the forest world find ways to benefit from our presence. Fat raccoons grow fatter eating our corn and chickens all summer. One young skunk spent an entire spring sleeping next to the grain bin in the barn, undisturbed by our daytime habits. A milk snake, who preferred to keep cool wrapped around our dog's water dish, would not stay out of the house in spite of daily evictions.

Midwinter this year brought a porcupine. The porcupine, *Erethizon dorsatum*, does not hibernate, yet is not overly fond of snow. Once a cozy spot which provides warmth and food is located, he rarely ventures far afield. Our young Erethizon, as we were soon calling him, followed that pattern exactly. He established a den under our neighbor's cottage with a short, direct path to our towering, tasty Scotch pine. We did not have many trees along our shore and this one was a beauty.

One evening in late January, we spotted him munching away on the pine's bark, and within a week the tree trunk was stripped bare. We tried to capture him with a salt-filled trap. No luck. Shooting was not a desired alternative. But as the snow deepened, and the tree's condition worsened, we knew something had to be done.

One day, at dusk we five — my husband Pete, the children, and I — set forth, armed for the confrontation. Our weapons? A broken hockey stick left over from previous raccoon engagements, a wooden club, a seven-foot length of giant tinker toys, a garbage can, and a smelt net. We positioned ourselves in a wide circle to block all possible escape routes as we advanced on the Scotch pine. If Erethizon hadn't seen us coming, he certainly heard the nervous giggles, followed by shouts of "Quick! He's crawling down," and "Get him Mom," and "Where's the net?!"

Porcupines do not climb very gracefully, up or down. Their powerful claws do the work going up. Mostly they tumble coming down. It wasn't too difficult to scoop our porcupine into the smelt net. The harder part was keeping him there. Immediately he began hoisting himself over the net's rim. Four of us danced around, keeping our distance, yelling worthless instructions to my husband, the net holder. Pete put an end to our foolishness with a sharp command to get the trap. Quick!

We scurried back to the house and returned with our box-like trap, which at various times has contained raccoons, a skunk, several curious cats, and once thirteen chickens. It was the ideal spot for Erethizon. First, we dropped him into the garbage can, and then, with a tip and a push from the smelt net, our porcupine scuttled into the trap. The metal doors were locked, followed by five sighs of relief.

There remained one last adventure to complete our porcupine's day — a truck ride (I imagined it was his first) to a distant deserted forest where he could nibble away to his heart's content on some absentee landowner's trees.

Meanwhile, I am becoming aware of a gnawing suspicion that close by a groundhog slumbers. His sleep grows restless as he grows thinner with each passing day. Undoubtedly, he is dreaming of my fresh lettuce and pea sprouts. I think I had better remove the quills from the smelt net. I may need it come spring, and not for fish.

Robin snow
April, 1982

He sat quietly in the overstuffed chair, a soft, plaid shirt and knitted wool vest keeping him warm, for he was old and ill and needed these comforts. My little son Jacob and I had come to visit our neighbor, whom we called

Grandpa Bettle, and to bring him Easter bread.

He held my son on his lap and looked out the window at the gathering clouds. Much of his long life had been spent watching clouds. Weather was important in farming, and even now at 83 he watched over Black Angus and sold fresh eggs. Nature and growing things were a way of life for him. Before we left that morning, it started to snow, big white fluffy flakes that stuck to everything.

"A robin storm," he observed.

"A robin storm?" I asked.

"Yep, this is what the old-timers always used to call a robin storm — coming in April like this and all," he said.

My son and I arrived home to find our backyard filled with robins. The ground seemed to be littered with them, their brown backs almost white with snow. One particularly tenacious bird was perched on the fence post. From that vantage point he sang and sang, oblivious to the falling snowflakes. Spring's inevitable arrival was not to be interrupted by an April snow.

I telephoned my old neighbor and described the scene in my backyard. He chuckled over a "youngster" like me learning things the old-timers had always known about the workings of nature.

I am grateful for that day in April. I never saw my old neighbor again. He died before the month ended, before my son was one, but he left us a legacy for April — an appreciation of the robin above all other birds, a close, almost commonplace link with nature.

Three years have passed since my old friend died, but country ways are such that old people matter, and their friendships and impressions alter my behavior today. So it is as April comes again, I look forward to daffodils, but not until I've seen another robin storm.

Tastes like salt water
August, 1982

The two children, browned by the summer sunshine, explore the edges of the mud flat. Each minute reveals a new surprise as the tide slowly recedes exposing barnacles and mussels or trapping small fish and shrimp-like larvae in the pools formed by the vertical slabs of granite.

It is tricky business to negotiate the slippery rockweed. But hot August afternoons are not meant for speed so there is no hurry as the two carefully follow each other, stooping now and then to poke at a periwinkle or to rub the bottom of a foot bruised on a sharp barnacle.

"Just scream if you get cut, David, okay?" My daughter Jillian speaks with the surety of one familiar with barnacle cuts.

She moves on ahead of him, her pigtails swaying with her body's movements. Where the rocks and seaweed end, the mud slopes away quickly. Here floats an old handmade and weather-beaten dory. Its once steel-gray paint is now indistinguishable from its gray weathered boards. It is the perfect boat for summer make-believe.

"Hey, Master Marvel, hurry up," she calls to him. "There are two horseshoe crabs mating."

He gingerly picks his way across the rockweed mat to the shallow waters where ancient secrets of horseshoe crabs are preserved. The two dark-haired children peer into the murky water, the aura of excitement about them heightened by the prospect of stepping on a live crab. Their interest is short-lived, however. The sound of waves slapping against wood distracts them, and they scramble into the gently rocking dory.

They sit facing each other, afloat, but not adrift. Their security lies in the mooring rope anchored into the granite. She sits in the stern, playing at pirates and conquering the seas, assuming command. The sun beats down on the two buccaneers; the ocean is blinding with the sparkles of a thousand sunbeams. Yet the cool sea water beckons, and little ones cannot resist.

"I'm going in," she says.

Slowly she lowers herself over the stern into the inviting ocean. "Come on. You too."

Again, carefully, he follows her into the water, clinging tightly to the gunwale of the dory. She's been raised on this shore; for him today is a new adventure. He is getting braver.

"Hey, this tastes like salt water," he calls.

"You aren't supposed to drink it, David!" Her reply ripples with laughter and fun and just a hint of teasing, like the salty, sunny taste of August.

From my vantage point on a boulder a short distance away, I smile to myself and resist all temptation to interfere with their adventures. Hot August afternoons are the days of which summer is made. Summer is the time for friendships, and childhood builds on these experiences They will remain friends forever. I will do well enough to absorb this August day on my own.

A blackberry end to summer
September, 1982

I just left late summer behind in southeastern Ohio. With a lump in my throat, I watched a chestnut Morgan steadfastly pulling her Amish buggy along county road 260. An indigo bunting flitted across the same road and landed on a split rail fence bordering a meadow. Beauty in simple scenes.

Ohio's farmland, which gave birth to my mother and to my husband, is part of the soul of America. Charles Kuralt once said, "America is not homogenized yet." He had spent years touring these very back roads of a nation and knew that late summer goldenrod, corn fields, and cows, whose tails flick lazily at pesky flies, are as much a part of this country as the cities of steel, concrete, and industry.

Ohio's corn feeds the cows who in turn provide the milk for the productive Swiss cheese factories in the southeastern corner of the state. My ancestors settled in Ragersville, Ohio, and I never return without a visit to the local cheese maker. To spend a day in that small town gathering sweet corn at the neighbor's farm, swimming in the old pond whose resident bullfrogs keep me awake at night, and picking blackberries and avoiding poison ivy are all I wish to do.

That the land never changes, where kids still catch softballs in the field where I once played, is the reason I departed with a bit of sadness and a lot of pride in my heritage that contributed to Ohio's agriculture.

That word agriculture has universal impact manifested in a multitude of ways, and as I traveled east, I was soon pondering the variety and critical importance of farming in our lives. Pennsylvania continued Ohio's tradition by offering endless forests which opened to reveal immaculate, huge, and orderly farms. New York unrolled fields of baled hay bordered by carpets of purple loosestrife which left entire marshes blazing in magenta. But the land changed in New England as mass development's sprawl along I-84 left only empty and dilapidated barns while people rushed on. I was troubled by this seeming disregard for the land, but Maine and the few remaining weeks of late summer stretched ahead. I was home, and I soon found myself filling those days with the same kind of activity I had pursued in Ohio — farming.

My small son Jacob and I set off for the blackberry patch, a secret place to hide where no one but the red dragonflies and white-throated sparrows would know of our existence. This particular patch grew taller than either of us and was surrounded and overrun in spots with bittersweet, heavy with the still unripe berries that would be October's orange.

The blackberries hung juicy and abundant on the canes, and we picked with enthusiasm, ignoring the brambles and prickly bushes. I love blackberries — completely and without reservation. We piled the baskets to overflowing and sat together under a cloudless sky, imagining our kitchen on a snowy December morn. Surely we would have blackberry jam on such a day.

Yet blackberries alone do not mark the end of my summer. Asters are only beginning to blossom. Young goldfinches are learning to eat at my feeder. Middle Bay has never been warmer for swimming. But the real treat of summer is the promise of the country fair with its testimony to the nation's farming heritage.

And so it was that the five of us — Pete, Arek, Jillian, Jacob, and I — went to the Union Fair, and I found, once again, the farming spirit of Ohio transplanted to Maine. Vegetables, fruits, grains! Quilts, wool sweaters, wood crafts! In open-sided barns rows of Jerseys, Holsteins, and Angus, pens of Suffolks, Corriedales, and Dorsets, and varieties of fowl awaited our inspection.

I had not left the farming fields of Ohio behind. Climate and terrain have modified the conditions a bit, but the produce of the earth in its infinite varied forms reigns as queen of late summer no matter where I am. That is a comforting conclusion for me, and with it as my winter's companion, I can watch summer at last slide through my fingers.

Piggy Pork
October, 1982

Piggy Pork got loose last week. That was bad. But the events that followed, involving the neighbors, the radio station, and the police in our 25 pound red piglet's nature walk, were even worse.

However, Piggy Pork's expedition was not without benefit. It did give me a firsthand look at October. I never realized how tall the wild asters were in our meadow, nor how thick they grew. As I struggled through them, almost as hidden as my pig, I flushed a beautiful brown thrasher. Savannah sparrows flew with my every step. The autumn wildflowers were covered with bees. Blackberry vines grabbed at my clothing. This field was crowded, and somewhere in here was a pig.

Near the alder growth at the edge of the woods, a female towhee watched my frantic searching with amused silence. She was not making a fool of *herself*. I entered the far-from-silent woods, where every tree had its resident squirrel taking time out to listen to and chatter about a human voice which echoed among the pines, calling, "Here Pigg — eee Pork." Ah, what a day it must have been for those squirrels.

Chipmunks stopped to stare as I pushed on out of the woods and walked the lane toward home, listening for a snuffling sound. Dejection was coming on fast. How would that piglet ever survive in the wild? Would Brownie, who like a good little pig remained behind in the barn, ever recover from the loss of a pigpen mate?

I worried my way down the road to the edge of the last meadow, and there I found a fringed gentian. Not one, but several bloomed inconspicuously among the towering goldenrod and asters. Piggy Pork's escape brought me to this. I sat down and just watched the flowers for a while and thought about beauty and the peace of the day. William Cullen Bryant wrote a poem to fringed gentians; long ago in a hot Indiana schoolroom I wondered what that flower was. Now, I was sitting beside it.

The only sound I really heard when I was finally quiet was the humming of bees still gathering nectar for honey-making. I got up and went home for my camera. Some days it pays to chase escaped pigs.

Postscript: Piggy Pork, after traveling over three miles as the crow flies with who knows how many side trips in-between, came home in time for dinner without any help from me.

Twins
December, 1982

Sometime during that day I had heard weather forecasts of the coldest night of the winter, and at midnight, as I trudged over the frozen ground to the barn to check one of the ewes, those predictions seemed true. My breath hung in the air in front of me, captured by the bitter cold. Ice formed crystalline patterns, speckled with farm dust and dirt, on the windows of the barn. The wind blew the door out of my hand, and the slamming of wood on wood shattered the darkness like falling icicles.

Inside the barn, however, there was silence. The geese did not begin their usual honking ritual, nor did the sheep jump to their feet baaing for grain. Animals have a sense of reverence for the extraordinary, and their peace alerted me. From the far corner of the barn came the low murmuring of a ewe who had given birth. Anticipation and expectation had passed. On the straw in Shamrock's pen lay two small wet and soggy creatures who had only recently slipped into this world. The lambs, one black and one white, were so cold that amniotic fluid was frozen on their curly wool.

I was shivering from the penetrating cold as I entered Shamrock's pen and when I touched the black lamb's leg, the ice on it melted in my hand. Shamrock was making a valiant attempt to lick her lambs dry, but the night and cold were working against her.

I scooped up the black lamb — a little ewe quickly christened Daisy in hope of a spring that she would see — and began drying her with a towel while her mother worked on the other lamb. I applied iodine to her umbilicus and then repeated the process of dry and massage, dry and massage, over and over. Without consciously acknowledging it, I had made a commitment to remain in the barn and see the night through with this ewe and her lambs.

The white lamb — a ram named Arctic in honor of that night when the cold wind roared down from the north, freezing all the countryside in its path — got his massage and rub dry, too. I eased myself onto a pile of hay in the corner, and, as I held him close, his wet nose tickled my face. I kissed him in return, smiling to myself in spite of the late hour and discomfort.

In the light of the heat lamp my husband had brought, steam rose from the lambs' coats as the warmth penetrated. Pete milked Shamrock and fed her rich thick colostrum to the twins bringing instant nourishment to those new sojourners in the world of sheep.

All that warmth began to take effect. Shamrock's licking was replaced with nudging, and in an instant Daisy was on her knees, shaking her oversized floppy ears and then scrambling to her hooves. She took one, then two uncertain steps before toppling to the straw bedding. After that she needed no prodding to stand; her brother was right behind her. Without hesitation they nuzzled under their wooly mother. "Give us a little time," they seemed to say, "and we'll even find the right end for milk." They shoved until their tails, flicking in rhythm like flags in a breeze, signaled to this shepherd, "We've found milk. We are going to make it."

As the night wore on, I continued huddling in the corner of the pen, watching the newest additions to our flock. On rare occasions like these, December does descend upon the barn with the unexpected birth of lambs, a concern to the farmer. Yet somehow the lambing season, no matter when it begins, nor how long it lasts, or what inconveniences follow, is an event which captures the heart. The first and the one hundredth birth are not much different. They are all a wonder.

Midwinter on ice
February, 1983

I wasn't going to go along, but a bit of insistence changes my mind. Now I am glad.

The farm pond, a mirror reflecting sunbeams on ice and skate blades and electric fence wire, captures me. As I tug on my skates, I wonder why I ever considered staying in the kitchen. Midwinter on ice is entrancing.

I am not alone in that feeling of adventure and excitement. There are 16 of us, counting four horses and Greta, our honey-colored dog, who insists on staying on the ice in spite of her cracked and bleeding paws. Two of the horses keep testing the pond's solid surface, not comprehending what has happened to their water supply.

Each circle I make around the pond is marked by a nuzzle from the winter-coated palomino. Pal stands at the edge of the ice, chewing on frozen grasses and watching me as I sail past. Penny, the Shetland, stands beside him, and although in summer she is quite unpleasant, today she nips at no one. These horses do not belong to us, but in the delight of this morning, they seem to belong to all.

The seven children all skate with varying degrees of ability or with none at all, much like the four adults who take part in this pond madness. The young girl is a study in color, a kaleidoscope of stripes, none of which match, none of which really matter either. She swishes by, her long dark hair streaming behind her, her face flushed with speed and cold.

At the far end of the pond four boots mark the boundaries for the hockey-playing boys. Two boys are just enough to make a team, just enough also to let the rest of us know our skating is less than adequate to make the big leagues. We ignore their displays of sudden skate stops which spray us with showers of ice chips. My farmer neighbor Loren says that he will return late at night (when there are no teenage boys to watch) to practice his skating, dreaming of skills unattainable.

Not to be outdone are the little ones, slowly moving across the pond's expanse, tumbling, crawling, occasionally crying, but nevertheless learning to skate the tough way — on a farm pond without benefit of a smooth surface. If I had stayed home, I would have missed all this.

When the sun struggles to its noontime peak, we know it is time to go — the two older boys must head home against their will to clean the barn before lambing begins this month; the younger ones must go because their toes are cold and their noses running.

The pond no longer reverberates with shouts and squeals. The steady munching of the horses and the occasional loud cracks as the ice shifts, rearranging itself after our visit, are the only sounds left. The black and red kitchen chair where we change our skates looks very much at home, silhouetted on the pond's western shore.

The Olsons, our neighbor family, have left their sled with the smallest child's possession sitting in it at the center of the pond. Surely they will be back for him. A teddy bear, dressed in a bright red ski cap and wrapped several times around with a red, white, and blue fringed scarf, will not be forgotten for long.

I love this pond. In other seasons its salamander eggs and wood frogs, or cliff swallows and bluets, or still-summer reflections of sky and cloud have captured my imagination. Today its ice and sun flashes have held me again.

Skunk!
March, 1983

If I, like Rip Van Winkle, were just awakening from a lengthy sleep, I would recognize this month of March in an instant. I wouldn't even open my eyes. Lying under my tree, feeling the higher angle of the sun's rays, should give me the first clue.

The smell of awakening earth would engulf me, entice me to open my eyes and take a peek at this month: tiny pale green tips of daffodils pushing through the soil, pink and furry pussy willows beside the barn, bees leaving the hive on a regular flight schedule. Spring — on its way.

Yet I need none of these signs to convince me that it is March. Skunks and March are synonymous, and today as I walk around the barn, I cannot miss their nocturnal diggings and paw prints, nor can I escape the damp odor of the barn wood, which each spring releases the essence of *Mephitis mephitis*, a yearly reminder of Nosey, the skunk who came to stay.

We were aware that an 18 inch black and white creature was in the area. He'd been caught in more than one neighbor's garbage can, so when I tripped over him in the barn, I realized, after the initial screams of hysteria, that this little striped skunk had just found a cozy spot to stay. I, however, wanted him out — immediately.

My plan of attack was complicated in comparison to what I knew would be his very simple plan of defense. First, I alerted my neighbor for moral support. Second, I informed my children that it was possible that they would not be able to live with their mother if the enemy won. Third, I tied back every door in the barn to offer wide-open avenues of escape for both myself and the invader. Fourth, I secured the ladder to the hayloft as another means of escape, assuming that skunks don't climb ladders well. Fifth, I selected my weapon — the every-ready broken hockey stick — and began the offensive.

The little fellow by then had settled himself quite comfortably on a pile of wood chips near the grain cans, generally ignoring me, so that my first tentative, very tentative, poke in his direction elicited nothing more than a disgruntled rearrangement of his fur. However, my second strong poke forced him to stand which in turn caused my mad dash out the side door as I surrendered the initiative.

After a few tense moments outside the barn with nothing happening inside, I returned. This time without hesitation, I poked hard. The little skunk leaped to his feet, scrambled quickly out from behind the grain can. But instead of dashing out the door as I had done only minutes before, he trotted to the opposite end of the barn and squeezed under a heavy tool bench. I knew the battle had been joined, and the following hour was witness to an exciting (breath-holding) game of cat and mouse (woman and skunk) until both of us gave up.

Actually, I gave up. Obviously, the skunk did not wish to leave, and short of picking him up with my hands, I was not going to get him out. I graciously let him retire to his bed. Then came the irony. Promptly at sundown Nosey, as I was now calling him, awakened, sedately walked out the front door of the barn, and began his evening stroll and scout for food.

So simple. My problem was solved — lock up every door and window to prevent his return. But something about the little fellow's spirit had touched mine during combat. I decided to give him a second chance; maybe he would come and go like an unassuming guest and eat a few rodents to pay for his bed.

The next afternoon I returned to the barn with a greater degree of calm, expecting and finding Nosey asleep on his wood chip bed. I spoke softly to him, reassuring him that I only intended to measure the grain for the sheep, that I had buried the hockey stick, and that he could stay as long as he liked.

He did not move except to wrap his tail more closely around his body. Oh, yes, he did one more thing. He winked at me with one of his dark amber eyes. He knew a sucker for any sign of spring when he saw one.

Greta's death
April, 1983

April is a month of contrasts, an enigma, a month that often tugs at my emotions, pulling me back and forth between joy and sorrow. My forest walk is filled with crystal water, stray beams of sunlight twisting through the droplets, rushing down the small incline in the forest toward the waters of the bay, announcing the beginning of earth's release from frost. The sound of water slapping gently over pebbles seems like a roar in the stillness of an April woods.

If I want noise in April, I need to seek open meadow to hear the haunting clear bell notes of the meadowlark at dusk or the cattailed edges of a pond to hear the day long cry of the red-winged blackbird. It is at this pond, too, at twilight, that *Hyla crucifer*, the spring peeper, begins his mating call and is joined by the low quacking of the wood frogs, *Rana sylvatica*.

But here in the forest all is silent except for water skipping down the rocky slope. My feet leave impressions with each step, not like those on a sandy beach which are quickly washed away with the tide. These footprints are lasting, remaining in the earth, showing that I have passed this way.

My footsteps reveal my journey, unhurried, stopping to look under the leaves of trailing arbutus for early signs of this flower and farther along to run my hands across the top of a new rich-green patch of goldthread. At the top of the slope, I turn to survey the watercourse behind me. My telltale footprints are caught by April as she unlocks the earth.

Yet, frequently for me, this month has been a fulfillment of T.S. Eliot's poetic line, "April is the cruellest month…" That carefully memorized line did not leave my head today as I stood beside the newly dug grave. Our golden retriever lived through the winter and died this morning in April sunshine, which promised life to everything else.

My older son Arek found her lying near the head of the cliff, almost overlooking the bay, close enough so the sea breeze would have rippled through her fur when she lay down. April's sunshine always made her spirits climb, her tail wag a bit, her body put forth that extra effort to drag along her almost non-functioning hind legs. She's been walking often this week, to the end of the driveway and back. Seeing springtime promise in her eyes, I find it hard not to shed bitter tears over April's arrival.

Maybe the crux of the problem is that spring doesn't come quickly enough in Maine to ease the transition from winter. I have been spoiled by a girlhood in Indiana farm country, where lilacs bloomed in April and pear blossoms were pinned to the ends of my braids. In Maine, April stands in the way of all that color.

I think, perhaps, patience is in order. May is inevitable. Beauty will arrive, and loss and sadness and change will blend into my life experiences. The water does tumble clearly and cleanly down the forest hillside. Some days its message is just a little harder to accept than others.

Pink Tea
June, 1983

Pink Tea and Tiddlywinks. Pink Tea and Tiddlywinks. Those words, like the refrain of some half-remembered song which keeps tumbling through my mind, have a vague connection to this June morning, but for the moment I haven't time to follow the thoughts. I am about to pursue a friendship with this month as if it were a longtime companion, colorful, brimming with life and with varied topics of conversation, rich with the good smells of lilacs and fresh bread, offering solitude or multitudes as my mood requires.

I am on my way to Esther's cabin, tucked in a grove of white pine and oak, perched almost precariously at the top of a bank overlooking the bay. The dew on wild strawberry blossoms acts as a prism reflecting rainbows around me. A yellow warbler sings from somewhere near the raspberry-colored crab apple tree, "Sweet, sweet, oh so sweet." The sheep's meadow to the west surely must provide habitat for a crowd of bobolinks who never cease their chatter. It is going to be a good June day.

My neighbor is to be my companion as well, although she will not be here. Today we have planned a surprise for her — a June cleaning, spring style. The five of us will open her cottage, scrub it from rafters to floor boards, shake out the paraphernalia gathered by mice who have spent a cozy winter. We will dust and restack the musty *National Geographics* and the somewhat mildewed novels with copyright dates of 1919.

As this June morning passes and we find ourselves uncovering more of the friend who lives here, I am gradually coming to understand that this woman is not my companion as much as she is my daughter's. I am reminded of Maya Angelou who spoke about creativity, that for the inner life to flourish, each one of us must be touched as a child by someone who becomes a guide. This elderly friend has spent hours with Jillian, reading, talking, creating, and that child has come to know this cottage, its treasures, and this woman well.

We have opened the intricate doors of an old Japanese cupboard which is full of secret panels and tiny doors hiding tinier drawers. Tucked in the front molding is a picture of the two of them celebrating June together over a cup of Pink Tea.

Pink Tea time was a special event. "It's hard to remember how she made it, Mom, but I know she mixed pink lemonade and ginger ale." This bubbling combination, not unlike the lady herself, was always served in a clear glass teapot with lots of ice. She had brought the tea cups from Japan at the end of World War II where she served as a nurse.

On another shelf we find a small butterbox. "Hey Mom, I am sure this is the box of buttons that belongs on the table." Yes, the butterbox is full of buttons — round, square, oval, shiny, dull, rainbow-flecked buttons — of interest to no one except a child and an old woman.

We arrange the Pink Tea table, cover it with a linen napkin, and place the small wooden lamb, which collapses when a child presses the base of it, and a tiny cup filled with red, blue, green, and yellow plastic disks at the center of the table. Tiddlywinks. Does anyone play that game now or is it reserved for an old lady and a young girl?

Perhaps, and maybe that is the most important aspect of this cleaning day. I have seen the value of a companionship actively pursued. Much wisdom and even longer lasting experiences and love are to be gained from a friend, be it my neighbor or this month of June.

Like my daughter, I, too, will slip comfortably into June's cottage. She won't flip all the tiddlywinks into her cup without my chance to enjoy them first — the buttercups and purple vetch that will grace my kitchen table, the barn swallows fledging in my hay mow, the strawberry juice that I will lick off my fingers. My bike and I intend to fly down her country roads with the air, smelling of freshly washed grass, blowing through my hair. I will even stop at the meadow's edge for an imagined cup of Pink Tea. It is only fitting to take that time with an old friend.

Tractor dreams
September, 1983

My son Arek was waiting. Something very special and important was about to arrive. "Guess," he said to me. Then he gave me clues: Deutz, Satoh, Same, Belarus, Zetor, Leyland. No idea.

He went on: Kubota, New Holland, Pasquali, White, Case, David Brown, Oliver. Getting closer. Hesston, Allis Chalmers, International Harvester, Massey Ferguson, Ford, John Deere. Got it! A farm tractor? Right.

The names have become complicated as the complex business of international trade and manufacturing has burst upon the agricultural scene. But in this young man's life, the names did not matter. They all meant the same thing — farming.

Early in his childhood he had learned to love the sound of machinery at work — plowing, planting, cutting, harvesting. His artistic eye had found great beauty in the order of a newly baled hay field, and he carefully reproduced these scenes in pen and ink sketches. His strong body labored as a "free" hired hand to any farmer around who would have him; he would do anything to be a part of a farming crew.

When he was only nine years old, he would rise before dawn and quickly finish his house chores. Then, with a book tucked under his arm, he would ride his bike to the nearest field. There he'd find the Farmall, a 1952 model, its battered leather seat still damp with the early morning dew. A swipe with his shirt sleeve and he'd plop himself onto the seat and sit staring across the gently rolling meadows picturing the day when he could drive a tractor on his own. Then, likely as not, he'd sit for an hour or two and read... and wait for the farmer... and dream.

This year as September came on, a time when the earth brims with ripeness ready for the harvesting, his first tractor arrived. This John Deere came complete with extras that allowed him to begin to learn the intricacies and capabilities of machine labor. He relandscaped a yard with a front loader and back hoe. He cut the neighbors' acres of hay grasses and wildflowers with an undermount mower. Soon he will dig a shed foundation — all of these accomplishments with this marvel of the agricultural world, a tractor.

All summer long these beautiful machines have been at work from Maine to California. As I travel the expanse of this country, I continually am amazed at the recent accomplishments in American agriculture due largely to the advent of the tractor. How did those early settlers ever bring this vast and varied land into the state of productivity that exists today? Surely loneliness, wild animals, and weather were not the biggest obstacles. Those men and women must have seen a vision. They understood the meaning of hard work and were not deterred by the magnitude of the task.

They, too, must have sat on a tractor seat, or before that on the broad back of a plow horse, or even on the edge of a split rail fence and dreamed dreams like my son's — dreams in which a plot of brown earth is transformed into a green growing richness, heavy with fruit or grain, ready for harvest under a September sun.

Sweet harvest
October, 1983

One last harvest of the season is about to begin. Golden October's arrival heralds the amber honey harvest, this one rich with a sweetness that is the fruit of an insect instinct, a harvest that man began millennia ago.

I didn't think too much about the history of beekeeping nor the implications for mankind (like the necessity of plant pollination for food production) when I accompanied my husband last week as he routinely inspected his hives. Mostly I worried — and kept a wary eye on any worker bee who, in spite of the calming effects of the smoker, saw fit to buzz a little too near my head.

This inspection required that Pete remove the top cover of the hive and then, gently with the aid of a hive tool (yes, that is its real name), begin to separate one super at a time from the hive body. Carefully he extracted a frame — one solidly covered with bees and brimming with honey cells capped for the bees' winter and spring use, or more, likely, for the finishing touch on a hot buttery biscuit on a cold blustery morn. As he checked the other frames, this hive's productivity became obvious. There was enough honey to feed an army, even if it totaled 50,000 individual bees.

The thought of that huge number reminded me of an experiment I wanted to try. Having just read that a healthy hive would send out about 80 bees per minute, the following day, in an attempt to check the hive's health, I cautiously approached the pine tree hive, so named for its location on the south side of a stately white pine, and stealthily slid into the niche between tree and hive.

I began my count. Scientists, however, would not consider it valid. The criteria were not explicit. Did returning bees mean those that seemed to fly out only a short distance and come back? How is one certain which bees have actually been counted when a handful appear to zoom in from nowhere? Was the same bee counted twice?

By the time I had counted 237 bees in slightly over two minutes, I had reached the rather quick decision that this particular hive was perfectly healthy and that my experimental conclusions would be important to no one except myself.

But as I watched I did learn a bit more about our bees. The division of bee jobs was obvious. One particular group headed directly east down the electric fence line to the sheep's water buckets. When I peered into one bucket a bit later there were fifteen bees gathering water. New bees were continually arriving as the full bees departed on the water-run back to the hive.

Another group of bees headed to the west following the long line of pine and spruce and then turned north toward the fields of remaining purple asters, yellow hawkweed, and red clover. The hind leg pockets of returning bees were bulging with bright orange pollen. A few bees just plain hung around the front porch of the hive, like teenage boys on a street corner. Indeed, that is what those bees were — the expendable drones who have only one task in life, to mate with the queen, a one-time job.

Inside the hive I knew that many other jobs were being performed — nursing, guarding, building, comb cleaning, storing, feeding, queen grooming. I thought about all that amazing activity and gave up my counting experiment. Better to lick the honey off my fingers and enjoy it than to try to understand it.

Primary form
November, 1983

At dawn his golden-red outline is stenciled against the awakening horizon. Massive black oaks provide the etched background for this sentinel. Frost-laden grasses bend, each blade an individual spike driven to earth by the oncoming cold. He is alert, carefully watching for signs of predators; then he is careless, hunting for grass that is still green and palatable.

He slips under the fence, his ripped and flopping ear catching for a moment on the wire. He shakes it loose and moves silently among the flock of sheep, his uninterested friends. In their midst, he can sit securely, his paws pulling at each long ear, carefully combing and grooming each one.

As the sun comes up, only his upright form is visible as he stands on his hind legs and surveys the pasture. He is a figure cast upon the landscape. His life is like November — a quiet beauty in which form predominates.

This rabbit companion of mine is half wild, half tame. His shape and movement are frequently all he allows me to enjoy of his being. Some days I can get no closer than the shadow which slips between fallen apples in the small orchard. At other times I am permitted to touch him.

November is like my rabbit. At times I am allowed to touch this month, to walk through it and hold a wind-driven maple leaf as if this act will allow the fading brilliance of that leaf's color to pass through my hands, adding its brilliance to my experiences. On other days I must observe this month from a distance. Caught behind glass windows, I see only an incomplete view of November's form.

It is, however, this very form and structure which create for November a character of its own, one not shared with any other month. Rain which beats against the window appears like drops in a child's drawing. Yellow apples tinged with shades of peach cling like Christmas tree ornaments to the skeleton of the gnarled apple tree. Each head of frost-darkened clover marks its own meadow location.

That which was once frivolous, extraneous, and embroidered forest, meadowland, and seaside with extravagance is gone. Only the skeleton and support lines of the natural world remain. It is this pen and ink drawing which nature renders upon the landscape that engenders in me an appreciative response to November. Ralph Waldo Emerson wrote in his essay, *Nature*, "...the primary forms, a sky, the mountain, the tree, the animal, give us a delight in and for themselves; a pleasure arising from outline, color, motion, and grouping."

Emerson must have had a wild-tame rabbit of his own. Surely he has stood where I do now and watched the shape of a beautiful creature as it dances, pauses, hops, and then slips through the carefully sketched stalks, stems, and blades of the dying chicory and plantain. At dusk he, too, would have seen the difference in the sunlight, the softening of colors muted behind the intricate black lace of the tree branches which cover the sky.

He knew, and I know too, that a rusty-golden individual rabbit provides these moments with their own beauty. I would never wish to miss November.

Six geese a-laying
December, 1983

I have been thinking about that line from the old English carol for a long time now, and I am wondering why anyone would give his true love six geese a-laying for Christmas. Six geese a-laying are more appropriate for one's worst enemy. I know. I speak from experience.

Years ago two fluffy yellow goslings moved into a small, fenced corner of our barn. We were novices in the geese business then and foolishly chuckled over the mess they created, attributing spilled food and water to youthful clumsiness. As the goslings grew, they no longer needed pellet food and began to forage for themselves. We expected that. Part of the soft-sell of goose raising is the economic advantage of these fowl.

The two geese, who had become large, white, brazen adults, made it to Thanksgiving, and one was eaten. That was the first mistake. No one on this farm had ever plucked a goose before, and the difficulty this presented carried the plucker far into Thanksgiving Eve as he sat in darkness on the porch working away with feathers swirling around him like flakes of snow. That young goose was delicious, however, so the preparation problems were overlooked.

We had inadvertently created our second problem. One widowed goose is a sad, lonely goose. So it was on a cold December morning that our farming neighbor Loren, who owned a flock of car-chasing geese (and who was also a psychiatrist and should have known better), appeared on my doorstep with a feedsack tied tightly at the top with baling twine. He smiled his innocent freckle-faced smile, wished me a Merry Christmas, and promptly departed. As his pickup truck careened down the road, his chortles and guffaws echoed across the meadow. The sack began to flop, squawk, and honk at my feet. It contained a gift befitting Scrooge.

Of course, life looked up for the brokenhearted goose, and these two, Loren (we named him after the farmer) and Alexandra, led a blissful existence — winters in the coop with the geese acting as top dogs, terrorizing any hen, rooster, or duck who crossed their paths; summers basking on the front lawn, swimming in my son's plastic pool, or terrorizing the three fair-haired youths who crossed their paths often, armed with giant Tinker Toy swords and garbage can lids for protection.

Along about March each year Alexandra would build a nest in a corner of the coop and lay eggs. Loren, the gander, stood guard, not even allowing the hens inside to eat until I forced the issue at evening chore times. The eggs, for some inexplicable reason, never hatched, but a lot of hoopla went into the mating, nest building, and incubating.

This year, however, Alexandra laid her eggs in a nest she built under a juniper bush, and one cool spring evening the fox took her home to be the guest of honor for dinner. Loren was disconsolate.

I, on the other hand, was rather pleased. Loren was now docile and quiet. I would worry no more about my electric bill. (Loren chased meter readers, causing on one occasion an incorrect reading of over $100.) The sheep would graze in peace. With wings outstretched and flapping, Loren had ridden around on a sheep's back, showing off for his lady.

But a few weeks of silence aroused a bit of pity in me. This sympathy I felt for my goose caused me to spend a day just sitting in the grass holding the gander, to no avail. He was heartsick. The solution? There were two geese left at the farm, Loren's original home, so I tucked him under my arm and carried him back. I was sure he would enjoy having a real pond, not a plastic swimming pool, for splashing. I knew I would enjoy a clean sidewalk.

We all breathed a sigh of relief — too soon. Three days later Loren returned bringing his two new friends with him, padding down the one-half mile asphalt road to our front door step. We caught all three geese and took them back to the farm pond. One half hour later Loren and company were squawking in the front yard. Back to the farm pond again.

This time the three followed a direct line to the sea, through a meadow of uncut hay that grew over their heads. At night we could hear their distant honking as they floated in and out with the tide. We were delighted. Our geese had found the perfect summer vacation spot — for a week. They soon tired of the waves and gulls and vagabond life; they returned to the cold, cement doorstep where they were cared for.

What next? We packed all three geese into three garbage cans so they could not see where they were going and took them to the second pond up the road where they could keep the Black Angus company for the summer. That day they almost beat us home. We admitted defeat.

I stand in my doorway now looking over the heavily frosted field full of webbed footprints, and I can think of a lot of good things about geese. Fox and geese is a wonderful children's snow game. The goose that laid the golden egg is a magical fairy tale. Mother Goose is part of every baby's nursery. What would Maine winters be without goose down jackets? Pecan farmers in the South use geese as weeders and fertilizers in the pecan fields. I even know of a brewery in Scotland which uses a flock of geese as watch guards. They never drink on the job, are never late for duty, and never complain about working conditions.

Maybe six geese a-laying wasn't such a bad gift after all. My husbandry book tells me that six geese a-laying should be good for about 12 eggs each. Goslings sell for $2.50 in the spring. That's about 72 geese for $180. Not bad.

Or maybe I should stop fretting over this goose situation and face Loren eye to eye. Either he shapes up or I shall apply an old Christmas tradition. He may find that he has cooked his own goose.

Out like a lamb
March, 1984

March and lambs frisking on a hillside belong together, but it is not always easy to reach that day when March goes out like a lamb and spring is finally here. This year Bucko complicated matters.

Bucko moved in, just like that, without giving us a chance to consider the questionable benefits of his residency. He seemed genuinely happy to settle in next to the wood stove in the green plastic laundry basket. This home might be artificial — no comforting bulk of a wooly mother or sweet-smelling hay to nestle in — but if a lamb wants to be a member of a frolicking flock in spring, he'll accept any home to stay alive.

Bucko's mother, Shamrock, gave birth to him and his twin brother Bean in an icy pasture late one January day. She was a veteran ewe, successful mother of many twins, but this year she tended only one. When her rejection of Bucko seemed irreversible (stomping on, running from, and butting a bewildered tiny lamb are signs of irreversible rejection), we made the decision to bring him into the kitchen and to bottle-feed him.

His arrival caused very little disruption to the household that first night as he was too weak to even stand. The only inconvenience involved a 2 a.m. baby check to see if the lamb was still alive. Bucko's mouth temperature indicated he had warmed up considerably in eight hours. The next day confirmed it. Bucko was standing and when we lifted him out of his basket, he could hobble around on the linoleum floor in the kitchen. We felt a bit sorry for him though. He walked around the dining area, sucking on the ends of the tablecloth, examining table and chair legs as if they were the legs of his missing mother.

We were all very solicitous of the little fellow when he went hunting for his mother and quickly cuddled him and shoved a warm bottle in his mouth, murmuring phrases like "Poor little Bucko" and "We'll take care of you." Soon enough we learned who needed the caring!

Time passed and Bucko gained strength and size daily. He didn't quite measure up to Bean, who had their mother's milk all to himself, but he was doing well enough. We felt rewarded for our feeding efforts.

Only now a few little problems began to crop up. Almost overnight Bucko outgrew the laundry basket, not in length and width, but in height. He discovered he could step out of his bed whenever he wished and wander around the house at will. The wandering itself might not have been so bad if he had been housebroken (which he wasn't). I could even tolerate a small lamb's accidents. But the upshot of all this freedom was that it went hand in hand (hoof and paw?) with the chaotic rompings of our also unhousebroken puppy, Casey.

As soon as Bucko jumped out of bed in the morning, Casey would hear his trotting little hooves and pandemonium would break loose — an all-out white lamb-golden retriever scrimmage in the kitchen. Bucko had to be restrained. So the laundry basket was returned to its former function, and a new bed was resurrected from an old Halloween costume. Having lost his mobility, Bucko was a bit subdued for a few days sitting in an ex-robot, but we tried to make it up to him by giving him play time in the barnyard.

All six barn lambs were old enough to be outside for the day and Bucko seemed hesitant but interested in joining them. The mother ewes ignored him unless he came too close. Then a quick butt on the rump would move him along. When the lambs ran together in the field, kicking their heels or leaping high into the air, Bucko was in good spirits. When they returned to their mothers, he would walk along the edge of the fence coaxing Casey to squeeze under and provide a little in-flock excitement.

With Bucko outside for the day, his feedings were a little sporadic, but he continued to grow well. We still brought him inside at night, for warmth and mothering from all of us, but now it was necessary to lay a wooden gate weighted with two logs over the top of the box as he was quite good at hopping out of his bed as soon as we put him in it.

The night finally arrived when Bucko refused to go to sleep at all. He had grown just too big for a kitchen. I slipped my bare feet into my boots, wrapped my nightgowned body with a long coat, scooped up the rascal, and headed for the barn feeling much like a parent sending her child off to college — a great deal of relief tinged with a bit of sadness. Bucko would have to fend for himself.

And he has done that well. Oh, we keep bottle feeding him, of course. When we arrive, the other lambs all gather in a semicircle to watch the unique way that Bucko gets his milk. We enjoy having this tiny creature tag along after us, too. But most of all Bucko must feel a little bit special in this ovine world. He is a sheep, and he must surely know that, but somehow I can't help thinking that he would choose to frolic on a fresh green hillside in spring with a golden retriever at his side.

SWAT team
July, 1984

Eons ago the Fates got together to seal my doom. One of those old women, as she plotted seemingly capricious events for my life, came up with the bright idea of soft, appealing, but exceedingly clever raccoons as an all-purpose hex. I am a believer in that kind of uncontrollable destiny. My summers are now tied inexorably to the whims of raccoons.

Fifteen years ago the raccoons hereabouts were vegetarians. Oh, what they ate in the woods might have been meat — slippery newts, lively frogs, squiggly insects — but that was not my concern. The target of what I took as a personal attack was my garden's sweet corn. Inevitably the night before I intended to pick and freeze my year's supply of corn, the cry of "Sweet corn's ripe! Come and get it!" echoed from the meadow to surrounding forests. The vegetarians donned their masks, descended on the garden, decimated the crop, and grew fat.

The raccoons knew a "numby" when they had one, for every surefire trap I tried backfired. After ten years of being outwitted, I gave up growing corn. The raccoons regrouped and became carnivores. They now focused on barn raids executed by a well-disciplined and highly trained SWAT team of seven or eight ring-tailed sneaks. The team was well-organized and efficient. They knew exactly what to do to carry off their mission quickly and thoroughly. Their assignment: chickens.

I aided them in their thievery if I were lax and did not close the hen coop at dusk. Then they simply rolled out the red carpet and ambled up the walkway, joining the hens for an evening of festivities. On occasions they turned on the radio and added hard rock to the excitement. When I got smarter, I closed the coop door early. The raccoons in turn trained a crew of screen removers. Although entry was gained now with a bit of difficulty, there was in exchange the opportunity for an all-night bash without the fear of my arrival to shut up the barn.

My husband replaced the screen with hardware cloth, a harder commodity to remove. The raccoons were foiled, but only temporarily. They now entered through a window barricaded by hay bales. This new attack squad needed strong upper arms to toss the bales around, but again success was theirs. They even had a member, probably named "Fingers," who unlatched a bantam cage in a corner of the barn. Dinner that night was more like broiled squab than roast turkey, but adequate just the same.

After summers of various ingenious, but nonetheless unsuccessful schemes, it was with real horror that I heard my own voice ordering 20 chicks from the local feed store to be delivered in May. Why, oh why, did I insist on punishing myself and allowing my own fresh eggs to cost $3.60 per dozen to produce? When the 20 hens plus two free roosters arrived, I tried a new solution to chicken housing and the raccoon hex. There was an old box in the barn, a one-half inch thick heavy-duty wooden box with a solid floor, which had once been the body of a terrific go-cart. The box would serve as chick brooder. Over the top I placed an equally heavy-duty iron grate with two tractor tire rims weighting it down. Of course, the poor chicks could scarcely move and breathe, and I could hardly lift the rims off to feed and water them, but at least the raccoons weren't going to have a free lunch. To make sure of that, this tamper-proof package was placed in the closed garage. I did overlook one small problem.

The coons did not.

On the west side of the garage, several rows of shingles had been removed for repair, leaving a long narrow opening under the roof. From their ranks the raccoons called forth "Slim" and sent him on a one-man hit mission. Squeeeeeeeze in, he did. We know. We caught him. Sort of. Actually, we saw him as he escaped. Five chickens lost their heads, and "Slim" nearly had his tail blasted to kingdom come. I'm not sure how he reported to headquarters on his near death. Reconnaissance had obviously been poor that evening.

As for us, we moved the chicken box to the barn. As of yesterday, there were still 13 adolescent hens pecking around. (After the death of the original five, four more had been picked off by sneak assassin raids.) Surely the survivors' days are numbered. This morning there were paw prints all over my bedroom window… just checking out the lay of the land and the temper of the local chicken raiser before raccoon hysteria strikes again.

Hideaways
August, 1984

Summer ought to be like the Norman Rockwell painting that is tacked above my desk and is seldom seen by most of us who know Mr. Rockwell from *Saturday Evening Post* covers or the latest greeting cards. The painting is of a girl, her young calf, and the 4-H judge. As he inspects the calf, members of her family and the barnyard look on in anticipation of the judging outcome. I was a girl like her in summer, without the cow, but with 4-H activities and secret farm places in which to play.

Summer was simple and delicious then, and I don't think things are a whole lot different for children now. Young girls still love to bake blueberry cake, or groom a calf for show, or play in a hideaway spot, out of the main stream of life.

It is those hideaway places that fascinate me. They are as interesting and unique as the children who frequent them. Years ago my neighbor Susie and I played in one of those magic spots on her farm in the brooder house, a tiny white building tucked in the back of a maple-shaded lawn. It was so small that we both had to stoop when we entered. By August the chick brooder house was empty and clean, a perfect play house except that it was temporary. Anything we set up had to be taken down at summer's end. The thought of dismantling was not a deterrent, however. We would resurrect old furniture from Susie's basement, borrow brightly printed feedsacks from her mother's sewing drawer to be used as curtains, tablecloths, and such, and haul a dozen stuffed animals down the road from my house to be our naughty children. Those days were the making of an idyll.

The brooder house may have been special to me, but I have seen other summer-delectable hideaways that make me yearn to play in secret places again. One is an ordinary attic. Once I climb the steps, I enter the world of an old New England inn. The two young girls who "live" here, my daughter and her best friend Kathy, have created an atmosphere where they play out the meanings of historical times combined with the ritual of coming into womanhood.

The inn's rooms are complete with books from 1819 and L.L. Bean camp cots, a fox fur stole from a generous grandmother and plastic champagne glasses from a modern five and dime. The ivory soap awaits its first douse of water in a small tin wash bowl, and breakfast is spread in the dining room on a red and white gingham tablecloth. This attic is a treasure of a place, and the two whose imagination has created this shall be richer for the experience. Their lives are bound together by playing together.

Play is an enricher and summer the perfect stage for the acting. The bamboo thicket which grows tall at the end of the road has never been a source of bothersome weeds to the neighborhood boys. It is known locally as the Bamboo Fort. Hidden deep within its confines are rusty buckets and pots, junkyard bottles, and make-believe cook stoves. This fort is well camouflaged and prepared for siege. Its secret exits are designed for silent escape from evil enemies. Interestingly enough, it is also the spot where the boys go in the spring to find the first jack-in-the-pulpits, which are carefully protected from the pathway of the natives.

Of late, the smaller neighborhood boys have taken to using a small stand of cedar and spruce as their hideaway, and the Bamboo Fort doesn't get the use it once did. That is part of the passing of time. Quietly, and justifiably, some things slip into the background. That which was once important is no longer so. A bit like the brooder house.

I find that my feelings about summers now are inexorably linked to the summers of 30 years ago. As I look back into childhood, I believe that hideaways were more than summer's fun. They were and still are a building block in the world of creativity, an escape to another planet, a journey to the center of the earth, or a step back in time to an era known only from a book.

The children of this generation still know the sanctity of a secret place where one finds companionship or solitude, and adventure. I can look into a child's attic and never again really enter the summer world of make believe, but I can say, "I have been there."

Ghost fog
October, 1984

The earth still holds summer's warmth, but the air above is cooling. With this seasonal change comes ghost fog, that eerie gray mist which lies in long winding ribbons in the hollows of the land or rises like silent puffs of steam above the warm waters of an inland lake.

Ghost fog. Its presence alters the appearance of an ordinary dawn as sunlight sparkles through the moisture leaving me with a sense of anticipation that something unusual is about to happen. At dusk, ghost fog blurs natural objects and distorts my perception of reality. I know something is hidden, kept secret, within the fog. The happening of Silver Lake was proof enough.

The lake water was warm, but the air at sundown had cooled rapidly, and we four wore jackets as we dragged our shiny red canoe to the lake's edge, leaving a silver trail in the already damp grass, as if a giant slug had passed that way. The canoe settled into the green water. We climbed in, our older son Arek and my husband Pete the two paddlers. Our younger son Jacob and I sat in the center. Our destination was the general store in the small town at the end of the lake. We were camping, a vacation from our farm chores.

This small town exists by virtue of its crossroad. On the southeast corner sits the general store, on the northeast the edge of Silver Lake and the post office. Several large culverts and a rock-lined run-off for the lake are on the northwest corner, and towering above maples is the belfry of the Unitarian Church on the southwest. Each way from the crossroad leads to a different sort of existence, but the crossroad itself is a timeless place. It attracted us, and so we paddled over to visit awhile.

By the time we left the store, our mouths and pockets stuffed with bubble gum, the evening sky had turned navy, obscured partially by the gray of the mist which now hung over the lake, enveloping insects and travelers alike. We set off with a bit of urgency to our paddling. We had left our daughter on the dock, fishing, and it was almost dark.

It was then, out of that almost darkness, that the fog released one of its secrets, a creature which swooped past my head, banked swiftly to the right, glided back above the surface of the water, and rose straight into the air, just missing the stern of the canoe. A bat — feeding.

One bat, I thought, does not mean anything, yet I hunched forward over my son and pulled the hoods of our jackets over our heads. Everything was quiet except for the rhythmic dip, swoosh, and pull of the paddles and the crickets' chirps among the grasses at the lake's edge. Few words were spoken. The ghost fog swirled silently around us.

Then the bat returned, accompanied. Suddenly bats filled the small space above the lake in which the fog held late-evening insects and homeward-bound canoeists trapped with no escape. The bats flew like the night, without a sound, their agile bodies twisting and turning as their effective echolocation devices zoomed in on insect after insect. Not one of them touched our canoe or us, but they flew within inches of our heads and then were swallowed by the clouds of fog, only to return seconds later.

There were 20 bats. Then I counted 30, 40, 50 bats intent on feeding, oblivious to the amazement and trepidation they were generating in the humans below them. None of us had ever seen so many bats. All of us were ignorant of bat behavior and what we might expect to happen.

But nothing happened. We simply paddled on with the swooping bats as companions. The fog's secret was now ours as well.

Late that night, snug and secure in our tent, we would imagine that we had survived a bat attack. But that was also a distortion of reality. It would have been better not to worry at all, like the child we had left on the dock. When we finally arrived at our campground, Jillian informed us that the evening had been uneventful with few fish, perhaps because of the unusual number of birds flying about in the fog. We never told her the truth.

The cycle of things
November, 1984

My old tiger cat, Scallop, is living out his last days. For a while now, it has been obvious that he no longer is the agile and strong creature he once was. Almost overnight his sleek, muscular body has become thin and bony. His gait is uneven, and his movements have slowed. His huge mittened paws which delighted us when he was a kitten now seem like oversized boots and impede his progress.

He will die this week, and I have come to accept that. It is fitting that his death occurs near Thanksgiving during my favorite month. November is the month which strips the land bare and demands that I look at it. It is now that I must see the land for what it is — my life support system — and I must respond to that seeing and consider my place in the cycle of things. The land is a support system for Scallop as well. From here he took much of his food — chipmunks, voles, birds — and from the land, too, he took his pleasure, soaking up warm sun, prowling in golden meadows, chasing dry leaves across a wind-whipped lawn.

An animal cannot reflect upon the impact of the land on his life. I can't presume to know what goes on inside a cat's head, but I do know there are things that bring comfort to an animal. I am no different than he.

Land has always comforted me. The beauty of trees etched like black lace against a gray November sky and the loneliness of upturned garden soil are reminders of the gift of the planet. If we listen to the earth, it teaches us to give birth, to live, to die. This is, perhaps, the reason for November's existence. It is this time of year, in the gray and bleak and bare season, that I must listen to the earth.

Years ago I could look out my bedroom window at a group of seldom-used barns, darkened by weather, sagging from neglect. I noticed them most in November, surrounded by the damp chill mist which hung heavy over the landscape. The hoarse cry of a crow, gleaning pieces of corn missed by the harvester, would echo around the barns and then travel across the field where patches of pellet-like snow lay caught between the stubble of corn stalks. Those barns are gone now, but the rich brown earth remains, that robust earth which gave birth to me.

Today the earth which supports me is quite different from that Indiana farm. Now I live along the ocean's edge where clay is the soil, and the land rolls to the salt water. Scallop's long sojourn with me has been here. In the past 16 years he has explored every inch of this shore and the oak and pine woods at its edge. Our last walk together was in October under red oaks shedding acorns that a kitten would chase, but which made an old cat stumble.

Now, at the top of the land under one of those massive trees, we will bury him. The land does teach us to give birth, to live, to die. I know it doesn't matter to a cat where he lies. It only matters to me that I know he will overlook the sun rising on the sea, secure on the land he and I both loved. Thankfulness is knowing we have shared those things together. Sadness is letting him go.

Hunger Moon
February, 1985

Hunger Moon. Those words make me shiver. Winter Moon. I open the door quietly and listen, a bit apprehensively, for the muffled footsteps of a tomten, that sprite of Swedish myth and cousin to a gnome, stealing around the corner of the barn, while a midwinter moon watches over his activities. February nights and moonshine are filled with mystery.

Movement at my side startles me, but it is only my little son, insisting we go outside together. He says that it has never been so bright outside. He assures me that I will be glad to be in the snow. He persists and hands me my boots. I give in. He says that I am the best mom ever and that I won't be disappointed.

He is right. The moon is full, perfectly round, a brittle ice-yellow color which floods the meadows under its chilling stare. Jacob and I discover sun-shadows attached to our feet in this moonlight. We are not common humans anymore. We have become enchanted, like tomtens who appear on winter nights. Our shadows, dancing with each other, play a game of tag under the frozen apple trees.

I whisper to Jacob that I would not like to be a mouse tonight. This evening is a predator's dream. He and I feel eyes watching our antics, but we are big and safe from owls and foxes. A tiny white-footed mouse is not. We find the traces of a drama in the hollow where the cinnamon ferns grow in summer. There, the outlines of a barred owl's wing tips are pressed upon the face of the snow, the tail feathers fanned behind the wings. Seven footprints leave the point of impact and then vanish into the air. We try to imagine the midnight attack that occurred where we stand, yet only the moon knows the real story.

We gaze at the huge orb above us and wonder how many other people on earth look at this moon, too. Jacob's grandfather has told him how men of ancient China searched the sky to discover truth, but Jacob doesn't understand abstract words like truth. I try to explain that in China wise men believed that knowledge of the stars and moon gave them power over ordinary men. Jacob tells me he would rather think about moon cakes, not moon power. His grandfather has told him of eating moon cakes, a gift given during the Moon Festival in autumn. Now is the month for the Chinese New Year, another celebration of the moon's importance in Asian people's lives. Perhaps, Jacob suggests, we could make moon cakes now, here on this side of the earth, just to celebrate our night together, and to remember his grandparents living on the other side of the world, but under the same moon. I agree, and as we tramp home, our shadows walking hand in hand, we make plans for our own winter moon celebration.

Jacob chatters at my side, but my mind is wandering. We really don't know much about this sky above us, I think. Small boys can imagine quick hops to the moon and rides to the next galaxy. But I think only of the small gains man has made as he peers into the cosmos. We have less fear than ancient Chinese astronomers, but more unanswered questions.

I try hard to concentrate on the child at my side and the magic afoot here on earth on a night like this one. Surely there are tomtens somewhere about, some gentle fantasy to ease my unrest. Otherwise, existence could, like February moonshine, make me shiver in awe of that huge expanse opened above me.

Gentle Richard
April, 1985

This morning as I stood silently at the edge of a fence, I glimpsed one of those encounters between two animals that even farmers seldom see. I had come to check up on Richard, an unimportant little rabbit, a shiny red-brown bunch of fur with a tattered ear. Actually, during some part of every day, I check on Richard. He is a lively little fellow, a character who belongs in a child's fairy tale setting for he is a magical, mysterious bunny who has no idea who he really is.

For one thing, Richard is a "she" who one day appeared in a parking lot in town. By a series of coincidences, she was rescued from the traffic, spent a few weeks in a kitchen and a few months caged in a science classroom. Eventually she came to reside in our backyard, in another confined space. She was rather overweight and extremely lazy from her recent months of pampering.

After her arrival, however, it wasn't long before the ocean vista and barnyard commotion began to look appealing to her. Cage life was dull and obviously there was much to explore beyond the bounds of wire, so one day I set her free. I did this with trepidation. Other rabbits of ours have lived free — but not long — lives. I was sure fat Richard would meet her end soon. In spite of that worry, I held to the belief that an adventurous short life, for a rabbit, anyway, was better than a long life of tedium.

Initially, I expected Richard to return to her cage at night, but it wasn't long before she made herself comfortable beneath a huge pile of uncut logs. After that, she never again passed a night locked up. During that first free winter Richard often spent moonlit nights sitting in the back yard alone. I wondered how she escaped owl or fox; I wondered if she were lonely. I noticed she was slimmer.

By spring Richard looked sleek and trim, a survivor by any standard. About the same time, her desire for companionship overcame any shy rabbit inhibitions she may have had, and she moved from the log pile into our barnyard. At first the other animals ignored her, but her gentle nature began to make an impression. The others discovered a creature who didn't hog the grain bin, didn't run about honking and chasing everyone, and didn't act like a scatterbrained chicken. This newest farm member was silent, polite, and ate very little. Richard soon became the most popular animal around. Even if there wasn't another rabbit for company, life looked great for her. Freedom, friends, and food were all any rabbit could wish for.

The only problem for Richard these days remains the identity issue. I am sure she doesn't know what she is. Between dusk and dawn Richard is a cat. During those dark hours, shapes move in and out of the hay shed or scuttle around the corner of the house. If I look twice, I see a long-eared rabbit and a long-tailed cat, usually one of our own calicos, playing a cat and rabbit version of tag.

As soon as the barn is open in the morning, Richard leaves the cat shadows for a waddle through the muddy garden with the four iridescent ducks and sleek white geese. The fowl look for worms while Richard hunts for fresh green tips of asparagus.

But these are only her fringe identities. By far Richard's best friends are the sheep. She eats with them, perching atop the hay in the very center of the manger. When it comes to grain, she has become so sheep-ish that she disdains rabbit food and eats only 16 percent molasses pellets. Standing on her hind legs, Richard drinks her water from the sheep bucket.

On long summer nights the sheep are her protectors, for she sleeps cuddled next to one of the old ewes in the middle of the flock. No fox could ever smell her there. In winter she still maintains her independence and refuses to come into the barn at night. Her days, however, are spent with the sheep, eating and chewing their cuds in the winter sunshine.

Now that spring is here, Richard has new young companions. Today she is a lamb. A dozen white and black lambs kick up their heels, quivering with anticipation, and race down the hill and back, a flash of red darting in and out among their flying hooves. Finally exhausted they lie together. This is the moment when I arrive at the pasture's edge.

Richard and a tiny white ram have moved away from the others, their noses gently nudging each other. They pause and hold their foreheads together. Yellow and orange sunbeams dance across Richard's shiny fur. Very slowly the lamb's front legs fold at the knees, and he lies down.

Richard sits near his face. Methodically she begins to lick — first the lamb's nose, then his mouth, then his cheeks, and at last his ears. She licks his ears on the top, the bottom, the sides even though she is forced to stretch a bit to reach the top of him. The lamb tips his head from side to side as if to help her at her task. She licks until the lamb ram is as clean and spit-polished as a little boy on a Sunday morn.

I am still captured by the wonder of this tender moment. I don't want to leave. I would rather stay here all day and watch Richard. This unimportant little rabbit has shown me that caring for a good friend may be the most important thing I do today.

Before color was invented
May, 1985

May was bringing forth its green in a day meant for walking, a day to look at this blossoming world with delight and wonder. May, my second favorite month of the year — and I was being given 31 days to soar like the tree swallows over the meadows and bubble forth like the notes from a French horn rushing in praise of spring in the North. I could become May, crisp and new and untouched, if I could only see it all over again, as if for the first time.

I took Jacob, who had just turned seven and who, like me, has a tremendous fondness for frogs and bluets. As we walked, we talked, and he spoke with the newness of a child.

"Mom, what was it like in the olden days before color was invented?"

I did not know what he meant.

"You know, all those old pictures are in gray, Mom. I wonder who invented color."

So I tried to imagine, too, what it would have been like if color had not been invented. It was easy to explain to him that color was a part of light, but harder for me to imagine a month of May without it.

Color was everywhere. In the meadow by the barn-red bus shed, meadowlarks fought for territory, thrusting bold yellow breasts at each other. We ambled down the road toward the pond where a male red-winged blackbird flashed his scarlet epaulettes at us intruders passing under his telephone wire. We stopped along the graveled road edge to pick a few delicate Quaker Ladies, the pale blue ubiquitous blossoms of May.

As the habitat changed, we left the open, greening fields behind for the yellow-green budding of the forest. Dark green pine and fir towered over the fragile pink trailing arbutus. Jacob and I got down on our knees to brush away brittle brown oak leaves to sniff these tiny flowers. I thought of silly things in life, like how many times I do the dishes and how seldom I get to smell a mayflower.

Above us, the soft olive, gray, and muted yellow of the Nashville warbler flitted through the trees. In the thicker forest, away from the road, I could hear the "quanking" of red-breasted nuthatches. I know a place in those shadows where soon the blood-red of the wake-robin trillium will burst forth splashing its color on the forest floor. Before color was invented — imagine what the world was like.

Gradually the forest began to thin, and a tangled cover of alder and chokecherry edged the road. We were going to turn around at this spot and head home when a brilliant flash of black and white caught my eye. Above us a rose-breasted grosbeak settled on a limb, his deep rose feathers sparkling in the morning sun, his song rippling from his throat like a rainbow of colored notes.

I wanted to stand and watch, but Jacob was anxious to return to the pond, and so we moved on to where the pond's blue reflected the tall sedges, the sky, passing clouds, and the rusting fence on its motionless surface. We knew that tucked in somewhere at its edges were inch long tan-colored spring peepers, but in daylight we had never found one. At night there would be the bright yellow-spotted black salamander swimming, mating in the safety of the dark, carrying on the colors of spring. One of the chestnut horses in the pasture eyed us with the vacant look of a horse who spends his life in a field. He did not care that we were counting the colors of May. But I cared, for his thick coat was another of the shades that no longer belonged to the olden days of gray photographs.

Jacob left me then and dashed down the road toward home. I walked on alone past the dandelions, harsh yellow polka dots on a field of green. It suddenly seemed so important to protect all of this color surrounding me. An unnamed, uneasy feeling, like the onrush of brilliance that is May, washed over me. I knew that man could make decisions that would leave the earth only gray again, the colors of concrete and nuclear winter. I felt as if I had to protect May's rainbow for the child who still marveled at the change that had come over the world since the olden days of gray. He had made it all perfectly clear.

Raiders, again
July, 1985

The raccoons have been watching too much TV. In keeping with the times, last year's SWAT team of seven or eight coop raiders has been upgraded. This year's squad is a more sophisticated and slick duo who have traded their black masks for the cool glacier glasses look. I suspect they use an abandoned rowboat (nothing as fancy as a Miami Beach speed boat, but then, this is only Middle Bay) to make their nightly raids to indulge their favorite vice — chomping on raw chicken legs.

Actually, the summer began rather peacefully with no dead chickens in evidence. We were lulled into complacency. Nothing seemed unusual as I ambled to the barn to close up the fowl. Arek and I had planned a quiet evening at home. He was going to watch *Miami Vice* (with no thought of acting in an episode) and I was going to read.

In the barn the chickens were perched in two neat rows, beaks to the wall, tail feathers bristling at my eye level. I counted 13 tails. Okay. I sorted out four bills that belonged to the two ducks and two geese nestled in an indistinguishable heap of white feathers in the coop corner. Okay, again. It was only when I reached to shut off the light that this topnotch burglary squad showed its stuff. Obviously, the element of surprise when confronting the enemy is crucial. They had it. The squad, which had been hiding in the hay loft, suddenly moved with all the derring-do so common to TV heroes, bounding from rafter to rafter with the skill of stunt men.

I was in a difficult situation rather quickly. These two already had the upper hand, and I hardly realized there was a conflict. Their girth and sharp teeth made me wary of climbing up unarmed to prod them to leap down, while at the same time if I remained on the barn floor and they continued to swing above me, I was afraid they would leap down — on me. This nice quiet evening suddenly found me in the midst of a no-win battle, and I retreated for reinforcements.

When Arek and I returned armed with broken hockey sticks, the raccoons' low rattling growls indicated their displeasure. They wanted an uninterrupted evening of fun. But now feeling a bit braver with a young man at my side, I climbed toward the loft, thrusting my hockey stick in the general direction of the raccoons' latest position. The two fellows moved, but also separated, one hiding unsuccessfully behind bales of bright pink insulation, the other climbing into the middle of a pile of used tires. This appeared to be the old divide-and-conquer trick at its best. It worked. I could play this game all night and still lose.

"Get the raccoon trap and the wheelbarrow."

"Ah, Mom, now you're thinking." And my son disappeared into the night.

The raccoon trap is one of those specifically designed to be kind to creatures by capturing them for movement to someone else's backyard. We had used ours frequently — and caught all the neighborhood cats and one skunk. On other nights, when the trap wasn't occupied by cats, an especially adroit raccoon would crawl in, keep the trap door balanced against his rear end, unwire the lobster which we used for bait, and back out with his supper.

My son arrived carrying the awkward metal box. "What do you want for bait?"

"I'm not baiting it."

"What?"

"Just load it into the wheelbarrow and lock its front door. Don't ask questions."

Arek was definitely confused, but he followed orders, eager to get back to the real *Miami Vice* in the living room. The vice squad above us continued to slink about, occasionally drooling as they contemplated their dinner. I ignored them now and began to snatch chickens myself, grabbing them quickly by their legs and holding them upside down at my side.

"Mom, have you lost your mind?"

I was standing in the barn door, a flapping chicken in each hand, demanding that the raccoon trap door be opened.

"I'll put these chickens in — you shut that door fast." Two by two, I continued to snatch chickens and stuff them into the raccoon trap right before the disbelieving eyes of the two cool, slick critters in the loft. The tide of battle was turning and I was finally coming out on top. The success of our tactics began to dawn on the raccoons as my son wheeled their entire dinner menu and evening's entertainment toward the garage. I went back into the barn, opened all the doors and windows, unplugged the radio so they couldn't even listen to some good tunes, and rousted the ducks and geese, herding them toward the house, too.

If those two coons wanted to frolic all night in an empty barn, they could, but at least they would go hungry. We closed all the fowl in the raccoon-proof garage and went inside to watch TV together, smiling.

Next morning we returned all the chickens, ducks, and geese to the coop. No one had lost a leg and except for a few bent feathers and beaks out of joint from a cramped evening, no one was worse for the wear... except my Volkswagen.

It appears that as the raccoons headed for their waiting boat, they had circled the garage and in the driveway discovered my car with the windows wide open. Big paw prints went up the side of the door and trailed across the seats. Saltine cracker crumbs were everywhere. The crumpled box and a few other unmentionables littered the floor. The passenger seat was cranked back into a reclining position and John Denver yodeled forth from the tape deck. Crackers with chicken liver pâté would have tasted better, but it wasn't such a bad night after all for two cool dudes.

Book II: 130 Acres

Halfway around the world
November, 1985

Five gnarled and bent apple trees stand outside my kitchen window. One has only half of its original self left since the hurricane passed through. The other four are meant for climbing — each has thick limbs close to the ground with only a few tiny, leafed branches near the top. The trees are old and do not produce much fruit. At least they didn't this year, our first living beside them. My kitchen window is new, an intrusion into this quiet forest, and as I watch from my perspective, I discover much about this untouched land in November transformation. This is no longer the ocean that I observe, but a thick, tangled forest.

Because I love November and its bleak, bare days, its occasional, fading sun, and its frequent rains, it seems to me that everything that happens in this month should be exceptional, even the ordinary. And so I have made a commitment to record and examine carefully the activity at my battered apple tree in November.

The feeders went up in September. At our oceanside farm we had no trees close to the house, so feeders hung at a far distance from kitchen windows. Now they are almost close enough to touch. I watched as the black-capped chickadees one by one whisked in, shouted back and forth to each other, and fed enormously.

A few days passed, and they brought with them a near silent fellow who usually hung upside down, scooted discreetly down a long limb, snatched a sunflower seed, and quickly flew to a cache known only to white-breasted nuthatches.

A week went by, and then one day a woodpecker began drilling away on the largest apple tree. A yellow-bellied sapsucker, that infamous bird, the butt of bird-watching jokes, was in my back yard! The intricate black and white patterned back with a splash of red and the yellow-washed breast feathers was splendid, and as I watched him, I had fleeting visions of myself as the proverbial little old lady in tennis shoes. Well... so be it, I thought. This is November — time for the extraordinary. I bought suet and hung it the next day, just in time for the hairy and downy woodpeckers' arrival.

The blue jays came next, bringing in their midst one especially raucous fellow whose tail was almost all white, perhaps a distinguishing characteristic among his clan. These jays remained a little aloof from the other birds, and they ate daily at the half-an-apple tree which stands a distance from the others.

When November finally blew in, one evening grosbeak and a flock of juncos accompanied it. Seventeen tiny slate gray birds moved like deer mice under the trees, gleaning what they could from the feeder spills, their scurrying bodies making the ground roll and swell like the sea. A pair of purple finches, royal and shy, appeared at the feeder late one afternoon. They came only once, but I know, because it is November, that they will return.

Then, when I thought this month could contain no more surprises, a letter came from half way around the world. My father would be here for Thanksgiving. It was almost as if all the bird activity, in its very simplicity, had been preparations for a most complicated event. There was much to do. I wanted to arrange a place by the kitchen window, comfortable chairs, where the two of us could sit and talk about birds and other larger happenings in the world.

But this wouldn't do entirely. He had to see this forest in November, too. The same things I enjoyed he would want to look at as well — the bittersweet patch with its overripe fruit, Christmas fern more obvious on the forest floor and along the old stone walls now that all other greenery is gone. He would want to see where the sheep will feed this winter and how well the old John Deere, moved from my brother's Ohio farm, is doing in Maine.

The rest of the family would spend Thanksgiving preparing a celebration — my sister and daughter would cook, my sons would set a table laden with evergreen boughs, nuts, and apples, my husband and brother-in-law would chop wood.

But my father, whom I have not seen for a year, and I would talk about this land together, walk to the barn to gather eggs, explore the stone boundaries surrounding these trees, and then sit quietly and watch the wonderful hubbub of activity at my five apple trees in November.

"Wake me"
December, 1985

"Please wake me, shove me," the note read, "throw me off my bed.... but not too hard." My little son had scrawled this message for me, knowing I would arrive home long after his bedtime. I tucked the note away with other bits of his childhood I treasure and tried to wake him — unsuccessfully. I didn't have the heart to shove him.

I got that note out again this morning and thought a while as I stood at the window watching the darkening sky, crawling in low and gray, heavy with snow, that I should be especially glad to live where I do. I thought I ought to recopy Jacob's note and send it to Old Man Winter as a reminder to usher this new season in with the proper fanfare but tempered with a bit of gentleness, too. Like Jacob, I would like to be greeted by this returning season, but softly enough that I can let the last of the warm days slip away without regret.

Winter with its howling winds and biting cold isn't my favorite time of the year, but I need to be wakened and reminded that a place where the climate doesn't change dramatically would lull me into a false sense of continuity. Life seems to just go on in those places, the same forever.

But life isn't the same, and this snow, with its tentative first flakes brushing past the glass before me, gives me a bit of a shove. It is time to venture out and consider my place in this cycle, time to get ready again for a change. That is a challenge, like being tossed off my bed.

I need to take a few moments, put on my old frayed and worn jacket, the one that has greeted the first snowstorm for 22 seasons, pull out the blue-striped cap that my father once took off his head and put on mine in a cold sheep barn a long time ago, dig out the mended, yellow mittens from a drawer, and walk a while in the first snow of the season. Beauty in the form of white lace and ice crystal is being dumped in my yard. If I wish, I can jump off my bed of autumn leaves into a pile of goose down.

January is the time to awaken to a bright sun and fresh snowfall. Today is the time to watch snow arrive with the building crescendo of the wind's blasts, the mounting sense of urgency of swirling flakes. I don't want to hear the children's cries for skis or skates or sleds. I would rather savor a moment or two of this first snow with only the sounds of the storm.

The snowflakes bite harder at the window, seemingly asking me why I am still standing beside the woodstove. Okay, I reply. I'm coming. If I don't go outside now, I will miss all the excitement. But one last thing — Jacob's note. I fold it carefully and tuck it in my pocket. It is my charm against winter. Maybe I think it will protect me from being thrown off my summer's bed a bit too hard.

The art of seed selection
February, 1986

A woman with a long braid wrapped around her head sits on an old rocker, the kind with a woven rush seat. With her back toward me, her feet propped on the edge of the woodstove in front of her, she sips a cup of tea while the kettle steams. The floor around her is littered with well-thumbed copies of seed catalogues — from South Carolina, Ohio, Pennsylvania, Illinois, South Dakota, Nova Scotia — bringing the news of this year's best varieties.

I do not know this woman — she is only a part of the woodcut that is this month's calendar picture — but I do know what she is thinking, for the artist has captured in this single picture the process that is about to unfold in my home, my friends', my neighbors'. The urge to grow things is upon us all.

I could be that woman, for I dream, like she must, of the month of May, but this year my dream is not the annual, ordinary escape-from-winter dream. I am not just ordering seeds. I am starting a brand new garden. There hasn't been a brand new garden in my life for 17 years.

I feel like I am getting ready for my first formal dance. I started thinking about what I should plant months ago. Then in December Rosie, a friend from Coopers Mills, came to visit. She brought with her pictures of her garden, a simple, neat, lovely garden which inspired me. Rows and rows of weedless vegetables grew in a rectangle whose perimeter was edged with brilliant red, pink, yellow, and magenta blooms. The garden looked not like one of those grown by English gentry or fine ladies with gardeners who do the digging, but rather like a garden her grandmother must have grown in turn-of-the-century America. I want my garden to look like hers, or at the very least to give me the satisfaction in its order and color that hers does.

In January I called Orie, an old friend of mine who lives over the hill. He came to visit the next Sunday with five seed catalogues tucked under his arm. We discussed where the new garden ought to be located — east side (the company side) of the house would be fine if I could keep it weeded, west side was better if I were going to be lazy. I will probably be lazy about weeding, but I chose the east side over his protest where I can watch the garden from my kitchen windows.

Today I pull my chair near the woodstove and, like the woman in the woodcut, have my cup of tea and catalogues before me. I have been devoting hours to my catalogue search, reading about every hybrid of broccoli, comparing days from seed to flower, resistance to disease, and size of yield. Do I really want Goliath or will Green Comet do?

I am fascinated by the catalogues and the seedmen who produce them. Gurney's, I discover, displays its seeds by an entirely different system — color and type — than Burpee's alphabetical order. Johnny's gives its gardeners keys to growth styles and history and even includes a soil temperature germination guide for each vegetable. Park Seeds' pictures entice me to buy everything. And there are more. The challenge of this seed decision matches any complex library research for a term paper.

Even if I finally come to conclusions about what to plant this year, the major question of "how to do" a new garden remains. Last week while cross-country skiing with friends, the subject of raised beds came up. Their backyard series of raised bed gardens, which began as an experiment, have become an integral part of their summer gardening experience — simple, easy to maintain, and productive. Now I have to consider that option, especially since the latest edition of *Organic Gardening* features raised beds. Can I integrate these and other new ideas into the vision I still hold of an old-fashioned garden enclosed by a hedge of flowers? More importantly, will my husband be willing to do all the hard work?

Thinking of flowers sends me to another section of the catalogues that I have resisted even looking at today. The pages overflow with a profusion of petals and foliage, making rainbows look sad by comparison. The scientist in me wants to consider the flower structure as the highest, most successful mechanism for reproduction and continuation of a species in the plant kingdom. The dreamer in me wants only to gather bouquets in a basket to decorate a home. Everyone's life should be filled with flowers, and I will choose more than enough for one summer.

Actually, the longer I work at this project, analyzing growth patterns and fantasizing about abundances, the more grateful I am for winter. Not only does winter illustrate the sharp contrast of growth and rest in the natural cycle, it also gives me enough time to solve my seed order problems. I surely can't make all these decisions in one day. The art of seed selection ought to be tempered by rationality, but it never is. Today I am sure I can grow everything — weed it, water it, harvest it, freeze it, eat it. Maybe I can. Maybe not. Either way, the adventure is just around the corner.

Spring fever
April, 1986

Webster's Wife came down with it first, and within a few days it had spread to Loren and Alexandra. The three of them together are rabble-rousers, and their behavior was exaggerated by the accompanying symptoms of the disease. They soon affected ten overbearing, black chickens and one little red pullet as well.

The immediate drawback to this epidemic was not the fever itself as much as the exhibitions that accompanied it. Emitting of high-pitched, incessant calls seemed to be the highest priority, followed by rapid wing beating and an increase in egg laying. The pullet, Alexandra, and Webster's Wife all made nests, two nests, for the three of them. At dawn there was a general exercise scramble, waddling or running, whichever was easiest, flapping and squawking twice around the barn. Then everyone raced for a nest. The pullet controlled hers. It was placed high in the hay pile and was, therefore, inaccessible to the fat, non-flying goose and duck. So Webster's Wife and Alexandra usually spend the day sitting together, each one squeezed a bit off center, on the one nest that contains both duck and geese eggs.

It is interesting that spring fever strikes even when there is no one of the opposite sex available (or worth considering). Loren has never fertilized an egg. Webster was carried off two years ago by the fox. Spring fever runs its course just the same. The ten hens who remind me of sleek ravens have no rooster either. Although a new fellow with rather extravagant feathers and a dandified air came to reside last week, he is limping around the edges of the barnyard today which probably indicates he doesn't quite cut the mustard with the ladies.

Spring fever in the barn is one thing, but when the house animals catch it, then I am assured of major catastrophes. The worst affliction this April seems to be Huckleberry Pie, our sweet, gentle, pink-nosed calico.

One peaceful afternoon she attacked our overweight golden retriever who was sleeping in the sunbeams streaming through the skylight. Huck marched up and swatted the rubber toy out of Casey's slack jaws. Casey's astonishment quickly turned to action as Huck came in for the kill, spitting and swiping. Cowering in fear, the horrified dog retreated onto the only apparent refuge — the double bed. The cat raced to the bedroom door, blocking all means of escape. The dog was surely destined to be cat mincemeat had it not been for intervention from a higher authority.

Huckle didn't stop there either. Her next opportunity for offensive behavior came the following day when she pushed my smallest son out of the loft. On the long flight to the bedroom floor, my child could not believe what was happening to him. His adoring cat with innocent green eyes had become a wicked rascal. Perhaps he was somewhat at fault for trying to push her out of the loft first, but just the same, no one around here messes with Huckleberry Pie these days. Spring won't last forever, and she'll surely get the summer lethargy soon.

All of this would be bearable if I hadn't caught it. Through the winter I survived all types of flu and colds. Viruses simply passed me by. But this week I came down with spring fever. I don't think I caught it from Webster's Wife or Huckleberry Pie either.

I was in a big barn down the road, one of those old, old barns with huge lofting ceilings for bats and swallows and giant rafters for roosting chickens. The center section of the barn was meant for wagons and carts, and each side housed, a long time ago, cows, sheep, and two work horses. As soon as I pushed aside the sliding door I began to feel a bit different, lighthearted. I sniffed the dry, dusty air, listened for the rustling of mice. I felt like scrambling into the hay mow with a good book. Instead, I skipped back and forth the whole length of the well-worn floor boards and thought about nothing.

I think spring fever is like tetanus; it can lie dormant in an old place for a long time and strike when conditions are right. Fortunately, unlike tetanus, the disease I caught in this barn won't last long. I am actually glad to have it, although I'm certainly not getting anything done. I have been watching two phoebes fly from tree to tree in my back yard for one-half hour. I did wash sheets and hang them out, but that prompted me to follow the path into the forest, tracking down a robin that sounded like a mockingbird. When I found the robin, I was compelled to check out the wood frogs who had just begun quacking in the small pond. So far so good. Spring fever is right on course.

Pshaw
June, 1986

Old month. My grandparents, Martha and Edwin, were married in this month in 1913. Old words. Grandma carried a nosegay. Old-fashioned lilacs blooming in her yard. Not high tech and classy. Just low key and easy. That's June, a time for an out-of-date stroll.

Starting with lilacs on my mind, I went birding last Saturday morning, and as I walked down the road, quiet with the early morning absence of cars, I started to think about old-fashioned words instead of birds. Words like *parsing* and *nosegay* kept skipping through my head as barn swallows skipped over the pond. Parsing. No one uses that word anymore or even knows what it means. I teach my students how to parse, but they don't know that word either. I wondered how many small children 100 years ago anxiously awaited the coming of June and the end of parsing. And did those same children bring an end-of-school nosegay to a favorite teacher, too?

Small students used to be the focus of my grandfather's work when he was only 19 and taught the young ones of Ragersville, Ohio, in a one room school house. That school house still stands on the hill where I played away the summers of my childhood, on the same hill where I saw a yellow-breasted chat, a warbler unlikely to be seen on a June Saturday in Maine. My mind again was not on birds but on Grandpa.

After teaching he went into the general store business. There the word *whippersnapper* was tossed around often enough. We young kids, always underfoot, were certainly young whippersnappers to Uncle Herman, Grandpa's brother, who was the postmaster as well as the storekeeper with Grandpa and, therefore, had more say in the matter of shooing us out the door. And if we weren't being whippersnappers, Grandma would certainly consider us *slugabeds* if we weren't up at the crack of dawn.

So in keeping with Grandma, and shunning the possibility of being considered a slugabed, I was up at dawn and found that birding was good this morning. The lure of yellow warblers singing and flashing their colors pulled me on down the road where I found chestnut-sided warblers building a nest and white-crowned sparrows feeding in the grassy lane of an old uninhabited house. Still, the fun of trying to recall unused words was my game for the morning.

Rounding the corner on my *shanks' mare*, I headed west. My husband told me that his third grade teacher always instructed the children to get on their shanks' mares and go outside to play. He was never quite sure what his shanks' mare was, and being as ignorant as he, I looked up those words in my dictionary. Hmmm. One's own legs as a means of transportation. A good mode of travel to use birding in June.

Ahead a beautiful sound floated from the woods' edge. I stopped and waited, listening and scanning the tree tops. With my binoculars I peered deeper into the forest, but the singer remained hidden, a mystery I couldn't solve. Rats.

Grandma would have said, "Oh *pshaw*," her favorite and strongest exclamation when life didn't go quite right. For Grandma that usually meant an empty water bucket. She would send my brother out the door with the bucket banging against his bare legs. "To the spring," she would say. Maybe along the way he would stop to pick a lilac or two. Grandma wouldn't have minded. June was her favorite old-fashioned month, too.

Got that summer feeling
July, 1986

I wait for summer the way a child waits for Christmas, with a squirmy sense of anticipation of green leafy days and brilliant, relentless sunshine. Summer provides such a wonderful change of pace. There is an ease about every event. Mornings hold no schedule; evenings last forever.

Every summer I have known has been a perfect season, flecked with bits and pieces of golden sunshine, sprinkled with blue, sparkling waters, dotted with splotches of purple and yellow flowers, orange birds, and dancing butterflies.

When I was a child I loved summer as much as I do now. And since I had lived a much shorter time as well, summers seemed to last much longer than they do now. I regret that. Not that I wish to be younger, but I would much prefer to come to the month of September feeling that I had languished in eons of carefree days, just like I did 30 years ago.

Back then, along about mid-July, my brother Jack and I would tumble out of a Pullman car in Beaver Falls, Pennsylvania, dragging our heavy suitcases, which would bang against our spindly legs, and run the length of the train platform to where Pearl and Harry stood waiting for us. I am not sure whether they were glad that two of their grandchildren had arrived with summer in tow or not, but we were surely glad to be in Beaver County.

Summer stood in sharp contrast to the only other season we really knew — school — and Pennsylvania, too, was different than Indiana, not flat and endless, but broken by curves and twists in the roads and forests that covered rolling hillsides. That was one of the joys of summer — things changed when you left the unvarying winter routine behind.

Grandpa and Grandma's white house had been an old cottage, spruced-up and winterized when they moved from the city, but the cottage flavor was still there in the back field where the outhouse stood, always freshly painted and probably the only three-seater for miles around. There was a real bathroom in the house, but the outback's primitiveness had its attractions — like the phoebe's nest under the eaves.

Beyond the outhouse was a forbidden piece of property, a field and forest that stretched for acres. As I think about that land now, I wonder why my brother and I, and later my little brother Jimmy and my sister Jill, never explored those fields on the sly. But we didn't. There is a family story that our father started a fire in that field one Mother's Day. He hoped to please his mother by raking leaves and brush into a pile; after he ignited it, by accident, a gust of wind came up and burned land from Route 151 to the back road. Five fire departments were called. Grandma was charged for their services. She paid and never told Grandpa the truth. I imagine that we didn't go to that field because Grandma did not want a repeat performance.

There were plenty of places for seclusion close to the house — the grape arbor with its twisted, climbing vines like crooked arms and arthritic fingers clutching at us if we wanted a good scare, or the willow tree with its mysterious, wispy branches that swished like the clouds in a dream, blurring the world outside and hiding us as we sat huddled near the trunk of the tree.

In another corner of Grandpa's yard was a hammock. Hammocks are awful things that have always made me seasick, except for this particular one. Here I would wrap myself in the green canvas sling strung between two giant trees whose names I never knew and sway to the hum of all the cicadas in the world. Those beetles were supposed to be the 17 year locust, but Grandpa's were something different, or had lost their ability to count, for every year they sang and sang and left behind their tiny, fragile exoskeletons, bizarre figures frozen in chitin, waiting to be collected. My brother and I, and our cousins who came to visit us, gathered cicada skins and piled them high for no reason at all, except perhaps to frighten Grandma.

One summer day melted into the next. We were always outdoors, swinging from trees or raking needles to make forts in the pine forest that Grandpa had planted between his house and Mr. Johnson's. Once in a while Grandma would walk through the meadow behind the pine forest to visit Mrs. Johnson and we would go along to see Mr. Johnson who was tall and spindly like a poplar tree and who had a wonderful way with wood. He carved toys for us — tiny benches painted red and white for tiny dolls to sit upon and bigger orange and blue wheelbarrows matched in size to my brother's cars and trucks that spent the summer in the dirt pile.

On other days Grandma went to visit her half-sisters who lived down the road, antique and ancient ladies, one big and hefty with a booming laugh and arms that engulfed me in one swoop, the other thin and fragile, with a voice like crinkling parchment, who wore newspaper close to her skin for warmth — summer and winter. I only went to see these great aunts when I had to, not for fun like to Mr. Johnson's. The doors to their houses seemed to lock in secrets, uncertainties about the future and complexities of past histories that were more than a ten year old wanted to know.

Back at Grandpa's the days stretched on, never rushed yet never dull, capturing the curiosities of a countryside teeming with life or the surprises of a house full of new games for playing and pretending. When Pearl and Harry surrendered us at the end of two weeks, it seemed as if we had spent three months in the Pennsylvania hills.

Years have gone by and summers haven't changed. Oh, maybe I don't hide under the branches of a willow tree anymore, and I do pay closer attention to the names of the trees and flowers and insects that fill my summer days in Maine, but otherwise summer is indeed a time of changing rhythm. I visit family and friends. I walk. I lie in the sunshine. I crouch at the edge of the pond and talk to frogs, or I sit on a rocky shore and watch my children swim in the icy saltwater. I weed gardens. I make jam. Most of all I marvel at the green lazy days that are mine for a time. And I wish summer would go on forever.

A single tree
September, 1986

In our farm by the ocean where we once lived, a magnificent sugar maple grew at the end of the driveway. I would spend a few moments on autumn evenings standing on the deck, watching the tree quietly, almost discreetly, surrender its leaves to the earth at its feet.

The tree began as a tiny sapling, not much more than four feet high, which my husband found huddled in a corner of the forest one spring. The maple was surrounded by taller, stronger trees forming the upper canopy of the forest, and, although it had grown to its present height, there wasn't much chance for a long survival. So he dug it up, brought it home, and planted it in our almost treeless meadow.

Overnight it grew like Jack's beanstalk, responding to rich soil, water, and lots of sunshine. A few years passed, and one winter a snowplow hacked off half of the tree. We took a roll of tree tape and mended the mangled branches, attaching them to the original trunk. We were hopeful but not optimistic for the maple's survival.

But it continued to grow, and soon it was difficult to mow under it. Some branches hung low, thick, and heavy. Others reached toward the sun until this maple towered over the garage. The tree became a favorite climbing spot of the children. From its upper branches, the offshore islands were visible. From its lower branches, the children were invisible, transforming the tree into a place of magic. I would come home from work and find two or three of them hanging upside down, rather like opossums, or swinging from limb to limb like a new breed of North American monkey.

Sometimes treasures were stored in a crotch of the tree. From one such space a tiny, pink bear disappeared, gone forever. The child who lost the bear searched the tree and the ground in vain. He missed the bear, but more so he (and I) were amazed that an ordinary sugar maple could make a pink bear vanish into thin air.

I am not sure why one tree can make such an impression in a life, but it seems to be that way. My childhood was filled with the presence of a huge linden tree that sheltered our backyard. All summer it peppered the ground with its tiny round seed pods which we gathered by the pocketfuls, for playing house or shooting at each other. I still have a handful of the nutlike seeds in a jar somewhere, one of those treasures which clutters my life with pleasant childhood memories.

And then just the other day I overheard Jillian say, "My maple turned red overnight." Her maple. Outside her bedroom window on our new farm grows a tall and rather thinly-leafed, red maple, not a tree that any child could climb or would choose for an adventure site, but a plant of certain potential. Now that it is red, dressed for the coming season, it has taken on an aura of elegance. Her tree has changed as she is changing with time and the season.

Yesterday my husband and Jacob planted another tree, almost an ironic gesture, for we live in the middle of a forest, not a meadow. But it was a wish of that boy to add a weeping willow to the plants that grow here. He only discovered weeping willows in August of this year. With a child's eye for transformation, he saw immediately the potential in weeping willow trees for pirate wars and Indian hideouts. He has his tree, planted next to the pond where he spends his summer, to build dreams on and to watch as the seasons pass.

The sugar maple where we once lived should be showing signs of the passing season now. I can still see it, for the most marvelous part of that tree was its color. To me, it seemed to be the entire reason for fall. The weather had to change, cool down, shorten its days so that this particular maple tree could reveal its true beauty — an orange more brilliant than an oriole, an orange that faded on the edges to peach and salmon and sometimes speckled itself with yellow-green blotches. The autumn sun, a soft orange itself, sinking slowly behind the tree created a surrealistic haze, a vision where, for a moment at the end of day, I could see all the beauty of the season in a single tree.

Hatchet day
November, 1986

Hatching day was May 21. Hatchet day should be November 26. It is just that we can't all agree if we really want to eat A.T. Not that we are squeamish. It is more that A.T., short for Attack Turkey, has wormed her way into the family, gotten herself a turkey-toehold in our affections, so to speak.

Last May, after we paid out a hard-earned $11.25 to the feed store, A.T. came to live with us along with three of her siblings, each of whom immediately demonstrated and confirmed all written instructions for raising turkeys. According to my homesteader's handbook, "Turkey raising appeals to the least number of people... turkeys are the most difficult domestic fowl to raise... turkeys lay their eggs standing up... they are easily frightened... susceptible to disease... and are amazingly stupid," or words to that effect. Cute though, at least at the beginning.

A.T. and the other three tiny, soft yellow fluff balls huddled in a grocery box refusing to eat or drink (my book warned me about this) because, as we discovered later that day, they couldn't find the mash or water which was directly in front of their beaks. Arek spent the evening holding each poult in turn upside down and dipping each beak first into the grain, then the water, then the grain...

The stupidity didn't stop there. When he stood each of the four turkeys in a corner of the box, isolated from the others, each held her position, facing the blank cardboard wall with an equally blank stare. They would have died there if we hadn't herded them together again.

The next night one did die — just lay down and kicked the can. The other three kept right on being dumb. After a week, the three remaining turkeys, who were faring a little bit better with the world, were moved from their kitchen home to the large upstairs bathroom where we organized a daily TET.

TET, Turkey Exercise Time, allotted 15 minutes of free-flying and romping on the bathroom's vinyl floor. The poults were still much too tiny to be outside. Besides, turkeys catch every known disease from chickens so they couldn't go anywhere near our barn. TET was a great hit until we noticed that two of the three turkeys each had a leg which would not stop twitching. Like miniature ballerinas, the little poults hopped on one leg while the other moved out from the body and back again, a turkey *battement jeté*.

When the turkeys grew larger and we moved them to a pen outside my kitchen window, the condition worsened. Their weight ended their dancing careers, and the hatchet, sadly, ended their lives. Our investment of effort and money was beginning to look like a mistake.

A.T., now worth the original price plus two bags of feed, didn't seem to care, or even notice that she was alone. Why should she, when life under the old apple tree was good and relaxing? Best of all she considered herself a house pet with all the rights and privileges. Each day throughout the summer I would let A.T. out for a romp, a little like the old in-house TET, but now she was really free. I would find her walking into the kitchen when the door had been inadvertently left open, and, much to the frustration of the drivers in this family, she also left daily deposits on the hood of the truck or car.

She took great delight in following me. My summer gardening days are filled with memories of a great white turkey standing next to me as I weeded or tootling along behind me for a walk in the woods. She had grown into a big animal with heavy, sleek, snow-white feathers and a head that didn't look too bad for a turkey. In addition, I thought her brain had enlarged slightly, getting a bit smarter, until the day she went to the garden alone and "got lost" on the other side of the house. Her cries — a half gobble which was snorted through her nostrils — brought us all running to her rescue. As soon as she saw us, she ran happily with outstretched wings to the arms of her keepers.

A.T. continued to cost us money as well. Feed disappeared at $6.08 per 50 pound bag, the most expensive medicated kind because otherwise turkeys develop blackhead, a horrid sounding disease. There were unseen costs, too. The day the tile-layer was working in our mud room (at $15 per hour labor cost), he disappeared. I found him supposedly cutting tiles but actually playing water-spray tag with A. T. in the front yard. More money down the old turkey tube.

When September arrived and apples fell, A.T. found a new diversion. Casey, our golden retriever, who comes close to A.T. on the intelligence scale, eats apples. So does A.T. She especially likes the apples that Casey is eating. That is nothing really new. All summer A.T. ate dog food, the big hunky-chunky kind. Casey, intimidated by strong wings and a fast beak, went hungry while A.T. strutted around with a bulging crop.

Once again Casey was never given a moment of peace. Fifty apples might lie on the ground and one would be in Casey's mouth — the one that A.T. wanted. She would sidle up to the poor dog, make a lightning fast jab at the apple, and Casey would be yelping and running for the house.

Things haven't changed one bit now that November is here, except that A.T. is plumper and better looking than ever. She still chases Casey. She calls to me every morning and actually seems to want me to pat her when she leans against my leg. Maybe she is smarter than I give her credit for. How unattached am I to this turkey now worth $6.50 per pound? Enough to eat her? Maybe I had better get busy and winterize her pen.

Strap on the skis
January, 1987

At last it snowed — and not just those little, wimpy flurries or stinging ice crystals of late 1986. The new year arrived with the fanfare of a royal court presentation with all its pageantry, pomp, and splendor. I felt an actual sense of relief when this storm came, coupled with a heightened sense of tension (just how long would we be snowbound?) and wonder in the face of a transformation taking place outside my door, shining white and clean, as pristine in its appearance as I somehow hope each new year will be.

So, Sunday morning shortly after breakfast, while dishes lay in disarray and Christmas wrapping still littered corners of the living room, I strapped on my skis and headed for the forest. Late this fall we had cleared two cross-country ski trails, and I wanted to baptize at least one of them. My brave, daring daughter and our golden retriever Casey had already ventured forth early Saturday morning, before the storm had blown itself out. She and Casey, who ran belly deep ahead of her, had opened one trail. In spite of ice balls that form between her toes, Casey loves running in new snow.

I wanted to try the newest trail. Out the back door — into my skis — over the small creek that had totally disappeared under a glistening cover — and westward to the barn. The sheep were massed together, eating hay, and milling around in the small space they had trampled. The south side of the barn opens to a fine paddock for wintering sheep — lots of sunshine and protection. But today, after so much snow, the ewes could not struggle through the drifts, some of which reached their shoulders. They contented themselves with restricted movement and fresh air. I, however, would not be restricted.

I entered the forest behind the barn, following my daughter's trail. There was such a simple beauty to the place. White on green with a blue sky, the only colors for the winter artist, enhanced this path where only days before dried and brittle leaves carpeted a dark, bleak woodland. Now the woods was full of tingling excitement, almost as if the trees themselves welcomed the physical weight of snow and were glad to droop low over the path.

Chickadees chittered, flitting over my head, carrying sunflower seeds to the tall spruce above me. In the distance I could hear the whistled slur of evening grosbeaks, yellow and black pigs going back for second and third helpings at our feeders. Far to the northwest where the trees are impenetrable, a lone raven called again and again, his hoarse, raking voice echoing off the hills. Some winter days this forest is very quiet; today it was alive.

I turned north, off the main path onto the new trail. I was the first to ski this way, but I was not the first one out since the storm. Almost immediately my ski tracks crossed a long run of hare tracks which followed the cleared path as easily as I did. Time and time again the hare entered the woody thickets to emerge some distance ahead of me, run the trail for a moment, and return to the woods. When I turned east again, on the spur leading to a deer yard, tiny mice and vole trails covered the open spaces. I found round openings in the snow where the tracks stopped or began abruptly, little round holes that mice pop through, tunneling down under the snow for cover and above it for a food search. These miniature paths swerved, circled, and zigzagged with a dizzying display of excitement. I could imagine those little creatures skittering across the snow. I wondered if they had as much fun as I was having, but I honestly knew survival was more their concern.

Later in the day these mice tracks will melt, blending one foot with the other, leaving a single, narrow line across the snow. Snow snakes, my children call these marks. Funny how snow snakes seem to be abundant after a winter snowstorm. My children will be glad to hear that snow snakes are out again.

Close to home, on the old woods road once used by loggers, the trees fell away from me and I no longer needed to duck under hemlock branches that stole my cap from my head. The loggers' road cut down past the old farm pond. I didn't even let myself think for a minute about the wood frogs buried in the mud somewhere close by. I didn't want to think of April. I was just so happy that it had finally turned winter around here. If the seasons are going to change, I have always felt they should do so dramatically, just like the beginning of this new year.

Fling open a window
May, 1987

I opened the window and called goodbye to Jillian, a ritual of ours that starts each school day. But unlike my behavior of the last few months when I quickly cranked the window shut, today I left it open. That act of opening a window, flinging my cares to the spring wind, was an act of joy. It was time to air out my house.

I watched my daughter climb onto the bus — and then I inspected the windowpane. It was filthy. Time to scrub those windows clean, to rid this house of wood smoke and winter's accumulated smudges. Healthy, invigorating spring cleaning and I were partners.

It is significant that I want to clean windows first. They are the essential element in the physical building that shelters me and my family. Windows define a home, making a room distinct and memorable. A puff of spring air welcomed through an open window ruffles a curtain or teases the blossoms of a plant on the windowsill and eases its way into my house and heart.

Windows invite light and air to come inside — and they invite me to step out. Sometimes the most impressive part of a day or a lifetime spent in a place is the memory of a window view. My childhood bedroom window was low, tucked under a sloping roof, a rectangular box with a wide windowsill. I could sit on the floor by that window, rest my elbows on the sill, and for many evenings just look at the nighttime sky. The whole world smelled wild and sweet and earthy outside that window.

In the daytime I would watch the activity at the two old barns, where wheat was unloaded, corn poured into the crib, and foxtail wild grasses blown by the wind danced among the rusted wheels of an old hay rake.

My brother Jack fell out of his window once, a window shaped just like mine, a rather dramatic event because he managed to hang on until my grandfather pulled him back in. I wasn't there at the time, but I never was foolish enough to open my window so wide that my whole body might fit through.

The most impressive windows in my childhood home were not the large picture windows with panoramic views of golden oat fields. Rather, they were the tiny ones that made life look simple and serene. The other window in my Indiana home that I loved was at the very end of the old summer kitchen, a shed-like building which had been attached to the main house and now contained a laundry room and a bathroom. This tiny window offered a view of a *Spiraea* bush. In early summer when it was heavy with clusters of white flowers, I would see nothing except a microscopic insect world as honeybees, bumblebees, and other six legged arthropods who drank nectar visited the blossoms throughout the long, hot days. In later years, when either my father had cut back the *Spiraea* or I had grown taller, I also had a view of the farmer's field which began less than ten feet from the window. Corn was as high as I was by the Fourth of July. It was a simple world.

When I moved to Maine and had a house of my own with an ocean view, my favorite window was a small, southwestern-facing one which captured a crab apple tree that overflowed in the spring with magenta blossoms, Baltimore orioles, and goldfinches. At sunset in November, the same window framed a network of tree limbs, woven like black lace over the indigo-blue of the sky. Nothing will ever remove those pictures from my mind. They were there for 17 years.

Sometimes, however, a window scene passed through my life briefly, and yet the memory remained. High in an ancient gray apartment building in

Pittsburgh there is a window that looks down upon a tree-lined street and an old stone fire station. For seven days when I was five I watched my grandfather disappear into that fire station door, swallowed by the cavernous building as if he were disappearing into a dragon's lair. A long time later I learned that he went to play poker with the firemen, but when I was small, I only knew the fear that through this window I had watched my grandfather vanish.

In Montana at a ranch house high in the Crazy Mountains there is a small window that overlooks a horse paddock. There at sunset a chestnut mare and her shadow-like colt frolicked against a blazing sky. At the base of a western spruce which grew south of the paddock stood my tiny, pigtailed daughter, watching, not moving — a witness to the wildness of the West. The window contained and defined that picture like a permanent photograph that stirs unexplained memories and wonderings: what did my daughter wish for, to be part of the wildness?

Time, in its fast-paced rush toward tomorrow, has let me look through many different windows. I have stepped into worlds not often given to man or woman because I stood at a window and looked just a little longer than I should have. A busy schedule has called me away, yet if I wait long enough, a fisher will run through a field or a redheaded woodpecker will pause a moment at the suet feeder, once only. I have windows to thank for these small gifts.

I live in a different place now, and as I spend my second spring in this house, I wash windows with care and consideration. It is too soon to know which view will be the special one, which scene I will watch through changing nights and days and then remember a long time from now, but I suspect my favorite will be the east windows, the ones I stand at now, watching Jillian leave. These windows capture the world of apple blossoms, the pond, the birdhouses, the sheep, the garden — and my children. This looks like a good place to start spring cleaning.

Windmills
June, 1987

One hot summer day when I was seven, Pop pulled the windmill down. It lay sprawled across the front yard like a giant skeleton pecked clean by vultures, waiting to crumble in the noonday sun. For more than 100 years that Flint and Walling windmill had clanged and banged, swiveled and creaked, buffeted by Indiana's capricious winds. Water flowed because of the gear system of that metal monster.

But for two years it had been a worry to my mother. Her imagination had created wild scenes of havoc — blades crashing into children's bedrooms (which never happened) — and more realistic worries of children falling into the cistern under the windmill (which also never happened, but could have). My neighbor Susie and I played house within the confines of the windmill's legs, dancing across the boards which covered the yawning hole, until Mom put a stop to that foolishness.

So Pop hooked the tractor to the windmill and, using a very long rope, tipped it over. He filled the cistern with debris from the log house that we lived in and grassed over the entire front yard. A few years passed, and no sign of the windmill remained.

My memories of that structure are hazy at times, but its hovering presence is an integral part of the first two summers I spent living in the country. I was only four when I saw the log house that was served by the windmill. We had come on a June evening when Indiana heat ferreted its way into every habitable corner, and there was no respite. Pop explored the property declaring it perfect for us all. I remember his "perfection" as skunk odor, burdock higher than I, lilac bushes, and a silent sentinel, the windmill, which towered over us all in that cicada-filled night air.

We came back the next summer to live. Mom was not excited. Pop was deliriously happy. The winter before he had built a cardboard model of how he imagined the house would look — someday. She told him he had five years and then she was moving back to the city. I am surprised she didn't move that July. There wasn't much in the way of comfort — no heat, no plumbing, no running water. The windmill only rotated; it no longer pumped. Children never seem to notice such inconveniences. Mom must have surely despaired. When Pop sold the outhouse for $15 and we had to use the cornfield, my mother took us to my grandfather's for three weeks. Maybe she considered never coming back.

But we did. All that summer, and for many more, I picked dandelions and plantain leaves and played house in the front yard. Tiring of that I would climb the cherry tree near the road, swing on its branches and eat the sour, orange-red fruit until I felt sick. Evenings I took my bath in the galvanized tub in the front yard.

My brother Jack escaped through the back field to Mr. Schlaudroff's barn, to stand in awe of the gigantic Oliver tractor which was usually parked next to the corn crib. Mr. Schlaudroff was kind to Jack. After all, this city family was living in the log farmhouse where his mother had been born. Here were new settlers on the land, and he — and our other farm neighbors — cared for us and supplied us with much-needed water. By August we had our own well and plumbing, and when Thanksgiving arrived, we even got heat. But the house remained unfinished for many more years.

Pop gutted the upper level of the house that first summer. We (there were four of us at the time, two more to come) were all sleeping, eating and living in one room, the main room of the log building. When the ceiling was removed, giant beams were exposed above us. There were mornings when my father climbed up among the rafters to chase away the birds that had come inside to roost. We thought the windmill was a preferable perching spot. Apparently the birds did not.

Thirty-eight summers have come and gone since that first windmill summer. In my travels now I spend moments pointing out working windmills, especially one just a few miles from our farm, to my own children. "See that? It's just like the one we had on Tillman Road." They grunt in response, but my children are patient and tolerant. They know, and in a grudging way, they appreciate what I am trying to say. Some things about life need to be passed on.

This spring when I stayed at my parents' new home 500 miles from the site of the fallen windmill, I discovered something old and familiar. In Pop's workshop under a heavy chest was a metal frame on casters, a frame made from parts salvaged from the windmill. Those angle irons forged 150 years ago in Kendallville, Indiana, that once straddled a homestead and supported the whirling blades of a windmill, were still at work, in another time and place and for another purpose. I smiled. Pop finds way to keep an Indiana summer going on forever.

Groundhogs and mothers
July, 1987

Groundhogs and mothers are honored in the wrong months. February and May have absolutely nothing to do with the activities that take place in July.

Groundhogs, also known as woodchucks or more technically *Marmota monax*, occupy every moment of the time I spend in a car these days. Their plump, broad bodies covered with sleek, carefully brushed, dark brown fur are the focus of my daily travels. While some people try to set jogging records for themselves, I am trying to set records for the number of groundhogs spotted peacefully nibbling grass stems along Interstate 95. The world rushes past them with all the fury that fear of a missed deadline or engagement can produce, and this gentle little creature stands, a bit bewildered, on his hind legs, blinking occasionally at the craziness of humans.

I have become quite fond of these little fellows. Reason informs me of the damage they will do to my garden. My grandfather's favorite picture of himself was one in which his feet were firmly planted on the ground, his left hand clutched a powerful shotgun, and a porcine-looking woodchuck fattened on the bounty of Grandpa's Swiss garden swung by its tail from his right hand. Other friends of mine spend entire evenings planting bombs in groundhog burrows, often to no avail.

But before the attack strikes home, I keep counting and enjoying this month of roadside woodchucks. I have learned where several of them live — one at the edge of the alder thicket where our road crosses the creek (a furtive, scurrying fellow who has learned to shuffle at a fast pace), one where the robins sing at Exit 24 (an observing groundhog), one on a locust-covered hill in my old neighbor's backyard (a guilty-looking groundhog). But more of them like to surprise me, popping up and then disappearing like jack-in-the-box toys.

Last week my younger son, who loves groundhogs, and I were driving on our gravel road past a rather quiet section of woods broken by the yard of only one house. As we came to the crest of the hill, we saw below us, huddling, unmoving in the center of the road, a baby groundhog. We stopped the car, inched ahead slowly until we were within a few feet. He looked up at us, startled, as if we had invaded a quiet summer reverie, and then, thinking further on his predicament, scurried to the side of the road by Jacob's window.

He didn't hide but resumed his huddled position and stared at Jacob, who had by now rolled down the window and was talking to the little fellow. This young groundhog's dark nose twitched, his eyes sparkled, but there was still a sense of disruption about his manner. I felt a little out of place, an intruder, now that I was actually face to face with one of these animals, and after a moment we drove on, leaving him to his solitude.

Surely, his mother came along shortly and moved him on his way, probably scolding him for his foolish behavior. No self-respecting groundhog sits in the middle of roads and communes with humans and lives long to tell about it.

The thought of that groundhog mother tending to her innocent offspring moves me on to other mothers, specifically the feathered one who spent this foggy, humid morning in a state of frustration in my apple tree. It was not a fun July morning to begin with when the female hairy woodpecker arrived at the sunflower feeder with one of her youngsters in tow. His incessant, "peep, peep, peep, peep, peep, peep, peep," which rose in pitch and shrillness and then subsided into a wing-fluttering routine, increased her vexation with this tiresome chore of teaching feeding habits.

She began with a lesson in sunflower cracking since my suet feeder is empty, and anyway, the resident hairys are quite fond of sunflower seeds. She flew to the hanging feeder. He followed her. She selected a seed and took it to her niche in the apple tree, a spot where long ago a branch broke away leaving a hollow, darkened opening where she wedged her seed into the wood and began to pound at it.

Meanwhile, the one who should have been observing and modeling himself after this behavior was lingering on the edge of the platform feeder and fussing with the empty hulls left behind from the tireless efforts of the female purple finches who have also been trying to teach their youngsters how to forage for themselves. The little woodpecker hopped around the feeder, paying no attention to the lesson.

His mother kept up her routine, making 10 or 15 trips to the sunflower feeder. On occasion he would follow her, begging to be fed instead of trying out his own skills. She would oblige, I could see, with an exasperated sigh, stuffing a kernel down his throat with a little more emphasis than was necessary. At that point she flew off to one of the distant apple trees. "Ah, where has my meal ticket gone?" the youngster shrieked. He followed her in an instant, and like most mothers, she returned after this show of independence to her maternal tasks of child care. This little scene played itself on until both birds had their fill.

Their departure left the feeders waiting for the arrival of the purple finches. In this case, the fathers came along, too, seemingly to ride roughshod on the rowdy flock. An important, richly-red father arrived, perched on a flimsy, unleafed branch of the only maple among all the apple trees, and with an air of pomp, prepared to oversee mealtime. His lofty and regal demeanor was promptly disarranged by the landing of an overzealous (and not yet well-controlled) juvenile. The young purple finch hit with such an impact on the same thin branch that the father fell forward as if someone had slapped him on the back in hearty congratulations for a job well done. He tumbled a few feet before remembering to spread his wings.

It is beginning to look like June should no longer honor fathers, either. July has a corner on the market for all the interesting events.

Frog patrol
August, 1987

The dog days of August are here... for the frogs. Every morning between seven and eight when lethargic green frogs, *Rana clamitans*, are barely able to stretch their cold and stiff muscles, Casey trots to the pond for her version of a canine-amphibian morning workout. For Casey, however, this athletic event has an all-day aura about it. The frogs are never safe until dark.

Casey's routine is consistent and predictable. If only the frogs would realize this, their population might not be declining. As it is, they may be in trouble. Casey's goal is to capture, and her approach is the same every day. Tail waving above her back, ears cocked, she arrives and begins, at a medium trot speed, to circle the pond. As soon as her shadow falls across the still water, the frogs should head for the dark depths, surfacing only for a moment's gulp of fresh air.

But frogs, being the creatures that they are, are not really a match for Casey — which doesn't say much for frogs. This is the same dog who cowers in fear of the turkey and the cat.

Her circling begins, her eyes as sharp as the kestrel on the wire above her.

Indeed, when she has spotted a ripple in the water, she immediately halts with her nose only inches above the pond. Casey looks like that kestrel, the two of them hunching their shoulders, imitating a Chicago Bear wearing pads under a football jersey. Like the kestrel, she has endless patience as well. A ripple means frog. She will wait.

Soon enough the ripple-causing frog makes a second move, a mistake. Casey lunges into the water with all the force of a tidal wave. Water splashes everywhere. Aftershock from her plunge forces the water boatmen, whirligig beetles, and water striders away from the shore and into the unprotected center of the pond where they dance frantically. Casey swims a short circle and returns to shore, her mouth firmly closed in a line of determination. She is thinking, "Next time."

But the person fooled is me. Once she is out of the water, a slight gag reflex sets in. She coughs. I smile, believing she got a mouthful that time. She did, only it wasn't water. When she coughs again, a sprawling, slick, green thing flops to the ground. Rarely is the frog dead — just stunned by the enormity of what has just occurred — Jonah and the whale. If I am quick enough, I can rescue the poor creature and fling him back into the pond to be caught some other day.

And so it was with a slight shock of horror last week I saw a great blue heron glide to the edge of the sheep's pasture, stretching out its gangly legs for a perfect field landing. Great blue herons were our daily companions a few years ago when we lived by the ocean, but they are a rarity on our 130 wooded acres. Another thought crossed my mind. Perhaps Casey was calling in the troops to intensify the pressure on the frogs. I got out the bird book. Great blues eat frogs, in fact like them very much — just another golden retriever in a feather disguise.

This great blue carefully picked his way out of the pasture, but paused at that point in confusion. The pond was hidden from view. What had been visible from the air now lay behind a slight rise in the earth. The heron turned right and stalked down the driveway. The sight was silly, even more so after he turned left onto the main road and, with the walk of Ichabod Crane, began a stroll to our neighbor's house. He went ten yards, turned, walked past our mailbox, and stopped. He considered the driveway for a moment, cocking his head to one side. Then slowly and deliberately, he lifted his awkward feet and paraded back into the pasture.

This time using a little more surveillance and lifting slightly off the ground, he discovered the pond at the north edge of the field and moved to the cattailed corner where his turn at frog patrol began. The evening passed, with the great blue fleecing the shore in tune with Casey's ambitions.

Their styles are different as they work the pond, but the frogs still worry. The heron is stately and silent. Like a stab of guilt or a flash of lightning, his beak snares supper. Casey is bumbling, splashing, overanxious in her approach.

But blessed with the same sharp eyes, she, too, is successful, not in catching supper, but in snagging a great bit of August dog days fun just meant for a golden retriever.

A mouthful of air
November, 1987

I came home from the feed store last spring with an active paper sack. Inside, two, soft bantam chicks huddled together in the darkness like the last two jelly beans in a discarded Easter package. We had not purchased our usual Rhode Island Reds for the year. Our flock was large and laying well, and although we are gatherers of a multitude of fowl, we had decided enough was enough.

But I am a big sucker for anything with wings, and the appealing qualities of these two had gotten the best of my better judgment. After all, I reasoned, what was spring without baby chicks? I had used that reasoning often enough (and if I didn't, someone else did) so that our farm has supported over the years seven odd geese, ordinary chickens too numerous to count, 37 ducks (some of whom insisted on drowning themselves in the sheep's water bucket), six quail, three mottled gray roosters (all named Lester), and an elegant white rooster named Chanticleer who was finely clad in emerald tail feathers, four turkeys (none of whom are with us now), and an assortment of bantam chicks who ran free and were usually eaten within a few weeks by a relatively clever fox.

Somehow the keeping of all these fowl seems more significant when the month of November arrives. It is this time of year when women's magazines bombard me with recipes for favorite dinners — roast turkey, duck, goose, or a tasty Cornish hen. I thought I ought to survey the barnyard fowl and perhaps select a plump roaster for a Thanksgiving feast. Easier said than done.

The black hens who once were the pride of my farm are all in a feather loss stage, embarrassingly so. Jill, my veterinarian sister, pronounces a vitamin deficiency. Phooey, I think. They are just molting, but in this stage of undress none of my hens seems suitable even for stewing. So, then there was Webster's Wife, the duck — that is, until last month when she died quietly in her sleep at an old age.

That leaves three unbearably obnoxious geese. Like overbearing matrons and a pompous businessman, they waddle throughout the dooryard, claiming ownership of rabbit food and sunflower seed, even pecking at the freshly-picked McIntosh apples. These geese deserve to be eaten, but their presence has defeated the local raccoons, eliminated the garden slugs, and kept prowling dogs at bay. I think we need the geese alive.

And so, I am left with the two little dust balls I brought home last spring and a skin-and-bones rooster named Blackie who is much too scared of the hens to consider joining their flock. He sleeps in the dog cage in the garage, but runs every morning at dawn to the barn to crow. He knows his place.

In contrast, the two tiny chicks have a secure position, worming their way into the heart of the smallest member of this family. No cute furry lamb or rabbit or puppy for him. Feathers have it all. Puff and Fluff, as they are affectionately called, believe a house is a home, and in spite of the cage they enter at night, an open kitchen door is considered an invitation to their true roost, a spot under the woodstove where they were raised.

These two little chicks, fully grown and weighing eight ounces, move about the front yard with the finesse of the fairies in *Sleeping Beauty*. They rearrange their tail feathers, which look like old-fashioned bustles, and hurry off to begin morning exercises and daily chores of bug pecking on the front lawn and under the hollyhocks. Fluff and Puff would only taste like the cream-colored cotton balls they resemble. A mere mouthful of air not fit for a Thanksgiving hors d'oeuvre.

So what *did* we raise on the farm this year for Thanksgiving dinner? Ground lamb on spaghetti squash? I am not sure what I will serve on Thursday, but I do know what we will not eat.

The heritage of lambs
April, 1988

It is dusk. The light is clear as the ruffed grouse winds her way through the cemetery stones. She startles me at the road's edge, a phantom bird appearing out of nowhere, running back into the nowhere of a graveyard. Further down the road the white water rapids of a tiny waterfall splash out of control over the tumbled edges of a stone wall. One spring, too many years back to count, someone built that wall. With hands calloused from work and a back aching from hours spent stooping and lifting, a man helped a fence to grow, marking the boundaries of a farmyard. It was a wall designed to keep in the sheep or keep out the neighbor's sheep, depending on the owner's perspective.

We have the perspective now of keeping the sheep in, and fencing is only one of the complex problems involved in a way of life that demands commitment to something other than ourselves. Lately, we have been spending a lot of time in the barn, not worrying yet about the fences but more concerned with the little lambs who will need policing come June.

This lambing season has been especially fine. Early January saw the arrival of five healthy lambs, tough and resilient, brave and bold in a cold world. Then came a hiatus of six weeks until, like spring itself, lambs hurtled down upon us with refreshing vigor. White, coal black, fuzzy, tiny, hefty, mewling, weak, brazen — they tumbled out into a new world freshened with the smell of an awakening earth, as the broom-like wind swept away the dregs of winter.

Unique in this year's batch of woolly ones are two who represent the extremes of the spectrum. Little Cassie, a large, leggy white ewe whose face carries the traits of her Corriedale father, square and strong, is the offspring of an old favorite ewe, Sweetheart. Perhaps this is Sweetheart's last lamb, for she is eight years old, a time for culling.

The significance of this birth lies in the parentage, the heritage from a line that may not have genetically correct traits for making money in the commodities market, but does have traits for winning the heart of this owner. Little Cassie's grandmother was, of course, Cassie, our first ewe. Old Cassie, dead for three years now, had been ours for ten before that. She was the first of the flock, the only real leader these sheep have ever known. She was one of those rare sheep with trusting eyes and a patient, calm manner, who follows the shepherd with a steadfast devotion. I have hopes that this little Cassie, born of a mongrel mother with ties to the matriarch, will give me another sheep to love.

And then there is Wrinkles, the ragtag, baggy ram lamb whose only devotion is to Jacob. The devotion is natural. Jacob provides Wrinkles with his nourishment. Ironically, Wrinkles is the elite of the herd, the only purebred Corriedale whose parents have papers, an official sanction like a duke and duchess. However, with nobility came a certain disdain for the common events of life, like childbirth; Virginia (the royal mother) promptly rejected Wrinkles and resumed her inert life of boredom. She is the only ewe who does not kick up her heels like a Scottish highland dancer.

Bottle-fed and cuddled by Jacob, Wrinkles is making it in the world, but only by the luck of the draw. Last week he completely disappeared from the barn. Jacob and I, anxious and somewhat distressed, slogged through mud and fought off the attack geese as we circled the perimeter of the barn. Calling his name elicited no response. A search of the hay mow was next, the place where Wrinkles and Jacob play together, often for hours at a time.

"I've found him." Jacob's triumphant voice had echoed through the rafters like a bat's radar, bounding off one beam and then another. In the mow I found Jacob's legs protruding from a hole in the hay pile. At the bottom of it, nearly suffocated, lay Wrinkles, trapped by bales much larger than he. Jacob dragged him out, and Wrinkles survived, no worse for the wear. My guess is he will survive for a long time.

The farmer who built these tumbling stone walls surely watched waterfalls and silent grouse pass over his land. He must have known the joy and concerns of caring for sheep, filling his days with special lambs who carried on the heritage of older ones, all of whom nourished the farmer and his family. That's a pleasant thought for an April evening.

Neighbors
June, 1988

If neighborliness could be packaged and sold on the drugstore shelf like toothpaste, would the manufacturers of the product find themselves with an increasing demand? Would we buy the product ourselves... or would we buy it to give away?

I am struck by the isolated lives "big city" people lead, not that neighbors don't still exist. They do. In good, caring numbers. But the loss of American innocence seems larger than what is remaining. Perhaps, too many of my family members or acquaintances have fallen into the no-neighborhood syndrome where they barely know the person next door and where, in time of trouble, there is no one to help. Whether these thoughts are accurate or not, the lack of a neighborhood strikes a chord of disharmony with me.

From where I stand, however, the sweet sound of harmony was made more acute this weekend by a genuine act of neighborliness that solved a problem for me. In a sense the person involved is not my neighbor; she works in my village at the post office. My problem was to get a piece of mail to Augusta. I wasn't moaning or groaning or complaining about the U.S. Postal Service. I was willing to take my chance on the swiftness of the mail. But this lady, who was driving to Augusta, offered her services instead, to deliver it in an assured, timely, and personal manner. An extra effort for her, a kindness shown to me. I felt good all day.

Then someone mowed a lawn in our neighborhood last week and didn't tell anyone he did it. The incident was a bit like the children's story of *Frog and Toad* in which each amphibian rakes all the leaves at the other's house, a neighborly gesture, and then hurries home feeling satisfied with the good deed performed. These Maine neighbors, however, were so pleased by the act that they asked everyone they knew until they found the 'culprit,' the giver of the gift.

Neighborhoods have a certain sense of cohesiveness about them, not tied by gossip or even organized social events. Indeed, they are sometimes more tightly bound by the wave of a hand. That is especially noted in my "neighborhood" which stretches for miles; from our farm we cannot actually see our neighbors. Yet down the road from me Bess, a dear woman, works in her iris beds, pushes her wheelbarrow, and waves and smiles with the enthusiasm of a teenager. Next door my son inquires about an old tractor, long buried in the garage; that neighbor Jack takes time to clear away the debris in front of the old shed and haul the tractor out so my son can use it if he wishes. We still have the tractor, years later.

A neighbor watches over our considerable farm when we are gone, even giving shots to a cranky ewe when necessary. I help another neighbor chase his cows back to the yard. At the crystal clear pond by the edge of the highway, a father and his son and daughter fish. They wave; I stop to chat a moment. They ask if my little son wants to join them. In the brick house the gardener Charlie gives away all his extra produce. Art, another delightful neighbor, offers his fields to be hayed. A special neighbor takes my youngest into her home to play anytime and offers to be on call when my daughter baby-sits.

Those of us who are blessed with neighbors know the feeling. One of my fondest memories, held now with a bitter sweetness because Lynn has moved to Iowa, is of her telephone call in the middle of a warm June day, when the meadows in front of her farmhouse were ablaze with the yellow of buttercups, the velvet purple of vetch, and the tickling swish of foxtail grass.

"The apple muffins are hot out of the oven," was all she said. She didn't ask if I were busy or too harried to come.

"I'll be right over." The meadow with its bobolinks and the farm pond with its barn and cliff swallows are etched forever in my mind with her smile and that sweet smell of apple muffins.

That same meadow was mowed for ten years by Bart, a neighbor who invariably took my older son Arek on his knee and taught him how to work a machine. The day came when that young boy drove the old sienna-colored machine himself, an International Harvester that in the eyes of the boy looked like a red-lacquered Chinese dragon puffing its smoke from unfathomable innards. Now that boy is a man who is buying the old hay baler from the same neighbor who gave a decade of his life to teaching him how to farm, and teaching well.

Sometimes neighbors become best friends — Kristofer, the little Norwegian boy who grew up with my small son spending every waking moment in each other's yards, Esther who summered in the cottage next door for 15 years and is now an intimate part of our lives. But neighbors don't have to be good friends at all. Small acts of sharing are the things that bind people to each other in a neighborhood. When my dear old neighbor Orie became ill last year, the four months of his dying were filled with the daily comings and goings of family, friends... and neighbors. Someone was always there to hold a hand.

What I love about living in the country is the opportunity for isolation and silence, yet the closeness of neighbors who physically might live a mile away. In spite of distance, they provide a wave, a smile, an extra hand when needed — that is the product that guarantees true neighborliness. It ought to sell like hot cakes.

Flashdance in the barn
October, 1988

On the first day of October with the sun bright and dancing and pushing the temperature into the high 70s, things started happening around the barn. In step with the unusual weather, shadows whisked in and out of the stacked hay bales as if they were October's will-o'-the-wisps. With the temperatures so far above normal, were we experiencing sunstroke? Secretive figures appeared at the outer edges of our blurred vision. Did we see what we thought we saw?

The night before the new month, at an hour long after the sun had set and with the full moon at least a week past, Jacob and I had gone to the barn to close in the chickens. The hens have suffered lately, victims of a raccoon raider who had been spied above the coop. Later he was found by two brave adventurers who, like soldiers of fortune, had set forth to tangle with him using a wrist rocket.

"I am sure we got him, Mom. I saw him lick his leg." Whatever happened, that raccoon had survived and was still a threat.

That evening as Jacob and I closed up in the dark, we saw no signs of wildlife. Only one ewe, who is confined to the barn, disturbed the otherwise sinister silence of the night. Then, the wind suddenly increased in intensity while we scrambled over gates, closing doors, checking nooks and crannies for chicken thieves.

We started back to the house. Leaves whipped at our feet. The wind tugged at our hair, our shirts, scratching us with eerie fingers. We held hands. Something moved behind us. Our flashlight beam found nothing. Only a rock on the road? A toad?

Then just as suddenly as it began, the wind died. Crickets repeated their calls endlessly in the now quiet night. Near the creek, where plenty of moisture exists, black insects rubbed legs and sang to each other in the autumn air. We laughed nervously and went inside.

The next morning, around the edges of the barn where boards meet earth, shadows flashed and danced again. But things look normal in the daylight, and near the purple wild asters to the north, we spied tips of tiny ebony ears wiggling a regular rhythm, betraying the small creature. A black rabbit, just large enough to fit into a hand and looking like a two-cent licorice drop, was nibbling on the wildflowers. He wasn't alone. Minutes later a ball of white cotton tumbled down the northern slope, red eyes gleaming like a demon. Then a gray brindled bunny joined the other two. What did we have running loose in our barn?

The answer was not long in coming. For more than a year now Bun, our lovable honey-colored rabbit, has lived free like our cats, coming and going as she (only we thought she was a he) had wished. Each morning she arrives waiting for food and an extra scratch before she goes on her way. Some days she spends hours lying in the flower bed, munching here and there but never causing irreparable damage. Other days she hangs out with the eight bantam chicks who scratch and meander through our side yard. Nights she frolics with the two calico cats, Huck and Pippin, playing a game of tag in the moonlight. Obviously, she does other things, too.

Like the cartoon light bulb clicking above our communal heads, the answer hit. Now we knew why Bun had looked much skinnier lately — why her dewlap was gone. Aha. Bun had borne barn bunnies.

Now the fun really began. No longer fearful of spirits and things that go bump in the night, we set up a bunny watch. Armed with gloves, net, and wool jackets (for snaring scampering bunnies) little children and one grandfather would sneak to the barn in hopes of surprising a handful of rabbits.

No one was very lucky the first day. Those little fellows (we think there are four of them) have a network of trails throughout the 800 bales of hay stored in the barn. They disappear in a wink, skittering along the edges of the foundation just out of our reach, giggling like mischievous children.

But today, when the first monarch floated over the deck along with the scarlet maple leaves, making it hard to tell one autumn sign from another, we finally caught a bunny. The brindled one sat in my husband's lap while we ate lunch. Keeping us company, the bunny ate a piece of lettuce and relaxed. Brave little fellow.

His nose and ears twitched, but not with the nervousness of commonplace rabbits. This four-week-old special is as new as the season and just as capricious. A true autumn bunny, unlike the Easter version, knows the ways of shadows and sprites — and how to add a sense of mystery and surprise to a rather ordinary event.

Land
January, 1989

The cold had lessened enough for me to consider taking an early morning walk. Icy wind no longer clutched at my lungs, clawing its way inside my body as it had last week, yet, the chill was enough to move my feet rapidly over the frozen earth.

I quickly checked the barn, slipping as I hurried across the thin slick of snow-sprinkled ice. The sheep stood, content, awaiting the season of lambs. January is a rather peaceful point in their lives. Cold weather does not harm them, and the earth has already done its job producing all the food they need until May.

The woods road from the barn to the north field remained snow-covered. Wind had not been able to wipe it clean, protected as it is by old pines that groan and snap in the early morning light. In such a brittle stillness, sounds traveled clearly and precisely. A hairy woodpecker repeatedly drummed his rhythm in answer to the rooster's crow back at the chicken coop. A ruffed grouse, frightened by my unexpected appearance in what had been a silent place for weeks, exploded from above my head and moved quickly into the thick cover of the trees to the west.

At the end of the woods road, the earth dips and is flooded by water much of the year, a swale-like area now covered with ice. Held in place by that ice, the prettiest part of sensitive fern and goldenrod, their dried fertile fronds and seed heads, stood or fell stiffly at odd angles like soldiers frozen in battle, while beneath the thick protection, nutrients remained frozen, waiting for spring to reactivate the food chain.

This swale is my favorite part of these land forms here, nurturing an infinite variety of plants and animals, and feeding Apple Creek which runs near the house. This spot must be like a New England rain forest where moisture, plants, and soil combine to create nature's endless varieties. It is here I find the beauty of a scarlet tanager in June, seeking his northern version of Brazil.

But now in winter the only sound here is a distant dog, barking his discontent at the end of a chain, the cry like that of an ancient wolf ancestor snapping at a frozen sky. I moved on — off to the north field to stand a few minutes and look at the land, a subject that has been on my mind for a long time now and has become naggingly irritating to me of late.

The north field rolls to the east, a clean, wide open expanse of acres that once fed a thriving mixed forest and now grows alfalfa. I know grouse lived here, for it was one such bird flying across this very spot which convinced me, believing in omens as I sometimes do, that this was the place to buy. Grouse can no longer feed here, and we are responsible for that change in the use of the land. True, the land still produces and sustains human and wild life, but in a different manner, and although this change could come about given years of succession, we interfered and changed the sequence of events.

Others have paid dearly for their roles in questioning or interfering with human use of the land. The recent deaths of Francisco Mendes Filho, shot by an unknown assassin for his stand on deforestation in Brazil, and closer to home, the death of a woman, shot on her land by a deer hunter, strike me as startling symptoms of the increasing pressure man is placing on the very part of our environment which allows for our survival. The land feeds, shelters, clothes us. We use it and abuse it as if the resource were infinite. It is not.

Witnessing a Maine clear cut allows the imagination to see Brazil's agony. One look in my own area can begin to tell the story of change. One town worries over tax pressures on open land; another debates the development pressures on a town water system; another sees irreversible commercial changes.

This concern for our planet is not new. Cries of warning sounded long before Rachel Carson. Thoreau lamented change in his brief stay on Walden Pond. E. B. White worried that man spends half his life "improving" his land, yet loses quality in the process.

We are among those who "improved" the use of the land. For some, this improvement is grounded in environmental wisdom. For others, the overriding concern is for material gain — witness the rain forest destruction. And for others, the unhappy choices seem forced, but inevitable.

We have been able to blame midwestern industry for acid rain and medical waste specialists in New York for polluted seas, but it seems to me that responsibility for the use of land has come as close to home as possible as our own communities now face decision-making with sometimes resulting fragmentation as we tackle the problem of how to wisely develop — or not develop — our open space.

Last week I drove by a piece of land that for 25 years has held one home and one family and one very large vegetable garden. Today a sign announcing new and fabulous house sites stands at the roadside. In one fell swoop one way of life is changed and replaced with another, a change that is not an improvement. The issues, including who owns the land, are complex and not easily resolved. Ultimately, none of us owns the land, but each has the power to destroy it. From the deer hunters' right to hunt to the rubber tappers' right to harvest to our own individual right to build a house, there are no easy answers. Difficult as it may be, however, this new year must be the time in which the world begins to find those answers.

I walked home from the north field in a spitting snow. I felt like spitting back, caught between my anger at development and my love of this land's beauty and open space and the realities of human existence. We, too, are perpetrators of damage, I thought. Land had been cleared here to pasture animals so humans could eat. There must be a place to find a balance in this matter, but I don't know the answer.

I only know that in my selfish way I want wood paths left for my grandchildren to wander and open meadows of buttercup and purple vetch for the next generation to see. I want undiscovered rain forest plants for medical research and air and water made for life, not death. I'd give up quite a few things in return for that.

Book III: Visitors

30,000 Cubic Miles
March, 1989

The large pond's center this morning is yellowing in the midst of an egg-white, frosted snow cover. For weeks, until today, the pond has glistened with whipped white icing. The only interruption in that blanket was the snow tubing trail, a remnant of my children's attempt to seek some sport in this drab winter.

But now the boiling, hidden broth is surfacing, and the pond is changing color. All that really means, I believe, is that melting time is here. The pond, along with all the earth around it, is about to release its captives. Water flows, and life erupts.

I am eager for that eruption. This emergence of water in liquid form — not ice or snow or sleet — is March. Last winter in the middle of the small pond to the north of the house, we found five tadpoles, probably young green frogs, trapped in water holes in the ice. They must have swum to the surface, fooled by the tempting, lying light of one December day when melting occurred for a moment. The tadpoles, unfortunately, were caught, prisoners in the midwinter ice. We tried to chop them loose, but the ice gripped its victims firmly. There was no release. Water exerted a strength beyond mine.

I walked the edges of the big pond carefully this day, looking for breaks, places where I might see other tadpoles who have overwintered or water bugs, wheeling their way to the surface after a too-long time spent in the dark. I stopped at the edge by the cattails, for only there could I chop my way through all the layers of ice. Water seeped to the top. I swirled my fingers through the cloudy mixture, feeling, sifting for some signs of life, but my hands could not tolerate the cold. I was pushing things.

Yet only last week I heard the first killdeer's cry as he whirled overhead in an open field, his voice echoing the water's answering enthusiasm for the change that is here. Amazing water — made of oxygen and hydrogen atoms, bound in such a way to produce this fluid that fills 65 percent of our bodies — gives us life on a blue planet. Water covers the earth in places to a depth of six miles. Its properties are unique. No other compound behaves the way water does.

In some ways it seems like a weak sort of substance. Flick it in my face, and it causes only passing annoyance. Let it run for eons and it carves and gouges great canyons in the strong, seemingly unyielding rocks of the earth's surface.

Our first farm was at the edge of a huge body of water, and for all its beauty, I was always struck by the power of water to destroy. Waves crashed; boats capsized and broke apart. Darkness and the ocean intimidated me.

But it isn't just the ocean. Last month, at the edge of the river in our valley, we walked in the late night down a gangplank to a smelt shack. Just as I stepped onto the thick, solid ice footing, at the river's shoreline a gigantic chunk of ice broke loose and smashed into the dark swirling waters below me. That old fear of water and darkness returned, and I retreated to the safety of land.

Water is power, but it also exemplifies life's soothing substance. Quietly, gently, water still trickles out of the spring at my grandfather's old house. Moss grows, mosquitoes buzz, and nothing threatens life at all. Fresh, earth-smelling, that same substance from Grandpa's spring quenches a summer's thirst. In mid-July we frolic in our pond, ignoring the late summer bloom of algae, basking in the joy of water.

The incredible differences in form make this month a celebration of water. It will rain soon, part of the spring resurgence that scrubs away winter. The amount? One estimate is that 30,000 cubic miles of such moisture fall on the lands of the earth. Unless there is a drought, we take this pretty much for granted.

I try in the month of March to not take water's release for granted. I want to see the pond open up, bit by bit, day by day. I want to see the streams run free and hear the peepers' awakened voices. Only then can I splash my way down a woods path and find the first wet and green signs of spring.

Baseball for Women
June, 1989

Baseball should not be called a man's game. I have been reading too many reviews lately of the film, *Field of Dreams*, and in every one of them, the writer claims baseball — and its dreams — belong to men. Well, they are wrong. I love the sport, especially as it is played on a grassy field somewhere in Iowa, Ohio, or Maine. I have loved the game since I was ten, and I know there are other women like me who share that love. Baseball belongs to us as well.

Last night I lay in bed, listening to the bullfrog twang his rubber band song, slowly asserting his power over the pond. A mosquito circled my head, landed, lifted off, came back for more blood, and I itched all over. It was 2 a.m. hot, sticky, like the feel of fresh paint.

I lay awake and thought about the evening. Two little guys and I had headed to the Legion ball game to take in a few innings before we went to the movies to see *Field of Dreams*, second time around for me. On the way home they told me that — what with the pond swimming, frog catching, woolgathering, baseball watching — it had been just about a perfect day. I thought so too.

This morning when the phoebe outside my window woke me, I started thinking again about this game. And I have come to a few conclusions. The love of baseball is determined by genetics, not gender.

My mother, who also likes baseball, is named after the best female player Ohio ever had to offer the world. At least that was the case in the early 1900s when Alta Weiss was pitching her way around the sandlots of the Midwest. Alta was a local hero, known as far away as Cleveland. She made the newspapers, and my grandparents held her in such high esteem that they named their first born after her.

Alta was no slouch. At age 17 she was signed to play with the Vermilion (Ohio) Independents, a men's semipro team. In her opening game in Cleveland's big league park, she wowed the fans with her fastball and curve. She even went so far, in 1907, to claim, "It's a little indelicate to say it, but I have also learned to throw a spitball" (or so the story goes in Ragersville). That's my kind of woman. For Alta's first opening game, which the Independents won 7-6, she wore a long skirt! But, thanks to local sports reporters, she was encouraged to appear on the mound in bloomers.

After Alta graduated from high school the next summer, she returned to her semipro team, now called the Weiss All Stars. During the season of 1908, they played in three states and finished the year with a .500 record. My grandparents' heroine was truly that. She played men's baseball (was even considered for the majors), while she put herself through medical school. Eventually she returned to her Ragersville home (my mother's, too) to practice medicine with her father.

Mom had close connections to the Weiss family besides the name. She knew Alta's father, Doc Weiss. He took her on house calls with him and later, when she was 11 years old, he taught her how to drive his Model T. Mom still talks about Doc Weiss and Alta. I even know what Alta looked like. How could I miss? The love of baseball is in the genes.

The genetic strand goes on, twisting and turning like a DNA molecule, refusing to let go of my addiction to baseball. I am directly related to a female ballplayer. Lois Youngen, my second cousin, was a catcher for the Fort Wayne Daisies. Part of my family's routine each summer, when the Daisies were playing in town, involved an evening at the ballpark to watch Lois catch. She was good, too, not famous like Alta, but good enough to play professional women's ball.

Then, when I was ten, one hot summer night as I lay in bed listening to the game from Comiskey Park, Mom came into the bedroom to turn off the radio. It rested on my maple night stand, a light reddish color piece of furniture which glowed with warmth and security, and now nostalgia. It had one drawer at the top, books on the bottom, and was just perfect for the bulky radio. I asked Mom whom she was rooting for. She answered, "The Red Sox."

"Okay," I replied. "Then I will be for the White Sox." She turned off the overhead light and sat with me in that close Indiana farm darkness, and we listened to the voice of Bob Elson call the game. I don't know who won, except maybe me. I had found a dream. A game with beauty.

The recitation of baseball's charms reads like a litany — green grass, blue sky so clear you can't look directly at it without tears in your eyes, an American flag, crisp white uniforms, a fluidity of purpose set in motion at the release of a ball, the crack of a bat. Finely-honed skills, but simple. Pitch, catch, hit, run.

The hype of modern baseball's problems doesn't bother me, except to make me a little sad for the people involved. The thrill of the game for me remains within the setting of the sport. The reality is that lots of little kids play it in the summer in beautiful places, real sandlots, sheep pastures, or front yards. Tucked away inside their minds are dreams, maybe to do with baseball, maybe not. Never mind. The diamond is the perfect setting for dreams of any kind.

The Little League team in our village has a bunch of dreamers on it, a female included. She's very good at third base. Who knows what will happen to the skinny kid in center field, the short one on second, the skilled one on the mound? It doesn't really matter. It is just that they are playing that game on a summer's eve with as much determination as they can muster. And lots of us baseball lovers, both sexes, in country or town, are sitting there watching… and maybe dreaming, too.

Tomorrow it might be spring
March, 1990

So — yesterday it was spring, almost summer even, with the creek running clear and the earth ready to stretch its nose and sniff, and then today it is winter again, with snow obliterating the world outside my window. The garden is hidden. The raspberry bushes vanish under drifts. This morning the bird house on the pole by the pond is just a bereft stick in the snow. Yesterday it was waiting expectantly like a young man in May.

That's the way it goes in Maine in March. Everyone says so. But I am not eager to accept the lack of green or of birds other than chickadees. I watched a great blue heron this morning — on television — stalk its way through a Florida swamp. I wished for a little action like that here. But in March wishes don't dictate my choices. Right now all we have are trees and pine siskins.

Making the best of those two things, four of us went to the woods on skis. There are two impressive trees in this forest. One, over 80 feet tall, is a white pine, probably 80 years old. Branches leave its trunk every few inches. It is a most unusual pine, decorated with long, thin projections which entrap a person in their intricate patterns. I am reminded of J. R. Tolkien's Murkwood Forest when I peer into the gloom under this mighty tree. In winter the snow dispels some of the mystery, but at night this is not a place to venture. Somewhere there must be a folk tale of trees who capture human spirits to fuel their own. This is such a tree. I am a little afraid of it.

The towering pine stands in the middle of the forest. But near the west wall, overlooking a highway at some great distance, stands a rock maple, gnarled, twisted, over 70 feet tall. Five feet over my head a cavernous hole has been carved into the side of the tree, eating its guts away, I suppose, but the tree is so large that it will die slowly, year by year, not in one season.

This maple is the porcupine tree, known, obviously, for its occupant, a smallish, sable-brown creature. He is usually at home during the day but seldom grants his visitors anymore than a view of his tail and the excretions which he deposits down the side of the trunk in an increasingly larger pile at the base. We make a lot of noise when we arrive — "Yep, he's home," and "Hey porky. Wake up," and "Should we go closer?" Such absurdities make us sound uncaring, pedestrian, foolish. But we say the same things every time we come to his tree.

And the porcupine gives the same response. His quills rise along the ridge of his rump. He pulls his tail under his body, and he sits. He always looks a little uncomfortable — to me anyway — with his head stuck up into the hole. I think he sleeps in a semi-sitting position, facing the hard wood of the rock maple. We notice that this season he has been eating his house. Great upper limbs are being stripped of bark at the extreme tips. He is a daring fellow. I imagine he has taken a tumble or two from such a precarious point.

Today we waited and watched him a long time, so long in fact, that he got tired of keeping his quills raised and finally lowered them into a normal position. My family, too, grew bored with porcupine-rump-watching and went on down the trail. Their voices faded into the distance.

The forest was very quiet when they were gone. I tried hard not to breathe. Trees creaked. The beech leaves, which refused to quit being leaves and fall to the ground in autumn, rattled in the slight breeze like parchment. A chickadee called. There were no other sounds. I was getting better at not moving. I waited. The porcupine rearranged himself.

Then, far off someone yelled, "Mom." The porcupine froze. Again, I waited. He began to squirm. A front leg inched down as he turned slightly. Then his nose appeared over his right shoulder. He didn't seem the least bit surprised to see me. He gave no startled response or quick raising of the quills. I couldn't see his eyes. They were as dark as his pelt. Only the round protruding mouth which he kept closed and his little black nose were visible against the dark background. Above his forehead, gray quills swept backward from his face giving him a windblown look.

I still didn't move. But he did. He turned and faced me. I felt a little uneasy. Now I was the intruder. This was his place. He lived here each and every day. I was just skiing through. His steady gaze forced me to go, so I nodded my head in polite greeting and retreated.

Back home it was still 16 degrees, not the 60 degrees of yesterday. Except for faithful chickadees, the pine siskins were still the only birds overrunning the feeder. Well, give it time. Tomorrow it might be spring again.

Cat's eye view
August, 1990

Today I have been crawling around in the grass, at eye level with the yellow hop clover and cinquefoils, pretending I am a cat. No one in this household is taking me too seriously, even though I am trying to convince them that this is important research: crawling-in-the-grass activity followed closely on the heels of floating-around-in-the-pond with my eyes just above the water level, mimicking the green frogs and the bullfrogs who look like dead logs, their legs extending behind them in watery suspension. I have been wondering just what it is like to look at the world from an angle other than five feet off the surface of the earth, so I set out to find the answer.

Cats get a much closer look at what is going on in-between the grass stems. I knew that, of course, but it seems like a profound idea when I am actually down there in the grasses, moving like a cat. First, I was swamped with tiny black crickets not more than one-quarter inch long who skip quickly between plants, avoiding the tread of a padded paw. They are not alone. Half-inch brown grasshoppers with just a tinge of green on the thorax spring in wild abandon from leaf blade to blade at the approach of an intruder. There must be hundreds of these hopping insects on one small hillside near the pond, maybe thousands.

I feel hidden when my eyes are at this level. Grasses tickle my nose, but I do get a close look at hop clover so that I can actually see the dying flower heads folding down, resembling hops, their clear yellow turning an ordinary brown. Rabbit's foot clover brushes my cheek, soft as its namesake. White clover grows in this spot, too. I hadn't noticed any clovers all summer until I became a cat.

Back in the pond, I like being silent in the hot summer sun, moving like a drifting piece of vegetation. To a frog, this business of floating all day provides opportunities to observe the comings and going of everything else that stops by for water or refreshment. There are, of course, the noisy humans who invade this realm, complete with large overblown plastic float toys that double as snow tubes in the winter. These people — my children and my nieces Jess and Kate who come to Maine every summer — splash and laugh and generally disturb the quiet of the day, but they don't tarry. Green frogs are not wary creatures, and if I remain quietly behind after my family leaves, I can float nose to nose with one, its sparkling golden eyes unblinking.

The bullfrogs and green frogs that inhabit our pond look up into a jungle much taller than the clovers of cat-walking. Here cattails make ladders into the clouds, towering like skyscrapers above a frog's head. Mine, too. The veins in the cattail leaves weave a crisscross pattern, an intricate stitching of green threads. If I am very still, blue damselflies and large black and white dragonflies will alight on a drooping leaf. They sometimes fly as fast as I can drive a car, eating on the wing and only pausing a moment to sparkle in the sun, just for the frogs and me.

In the early morning six geese, four white, two gray, waddle down the lane to the pond for preening and a short swim. Tree swallows swoop overhead, skimming the pond surface, clearing it of mosquitoes. Minnows, maybe young trout, swim near my outstretched toes, a little tickle, but the green frog still doesn't blink. It is only when the golden retriever arrives, looking for an amphibian snack, that the frog finally slips away, never betraying his position with his subaquatic escape route. Late at night, I will hear him, his croaking voice mixed with the bullfrogs' twang of loose banjo strings, interrupting the night cricket chorus. I know what their watery concert hall looks like.

At dawn there is another view to be had — the spiders of August, who each evening spin their webs from chicory and goldenrod stems, are hanging near the sheep pasture. Their view is higher than the cat's or the frog's, but from my vantage point, it is upside down. The beautiful black-and-yellow argiopes (*Argiope aurantia*), common garden spiders, are everywhere, their webs among the most delicate structures in nature. I wish I knew what their working day is like. I have never seen one spinning. Always, there are completed webs at dawn, the dew covering the silken strands making them visible and fresh — eight or maybe 28 webs in an area the size of my kitchen table. By midafternoon, in the drying heat of the day, I can't find even one.

I try imagining a spider's view, hanging on a web above the ground, tied from a switch grass top to the edge of a thistle leaf, with the sky at the bottom of the picture and my head toward the earth. Some webs are cupped like a concave lens; others billow gently like curtains draped from reed canary grass to sensitive fern to blackberry bramble. Each spider looks directly into this tall maze of meadow plants, patiently waiting for the arrival of a bumbling insect.

Like the spider, I waited a long time — long enough to count the circles around the thickened center of the web. The bigger spiders had larger distances between strands. The smaller ones had less than one-eighth of an inch between the almost concentric circles that formed their webs. Thirty-three times around for one tiny spider.

If it weren't for hanging upside down, I think I would like being a spider. I love chicory for the swiftness with which it flashes its glorious lavender-blue color in a morning blossom and then fades. I love the smell of the meadow plants, the taste of dew, the song of the crickets. Spiders have all of this.

The green frog, the argiope, my calico cat — all have a chance at their eye levels to take in these intricacies of August because they are willing to wait. Patience has its own reward. In reality, theirs will ultimately be a meal. For me, I have only to suffer the indulgent smiles of my family in order to see once more a flash of the short-lived blue damselfly or to count the threads in a spider's web or to wait with my nose in the grasses until I can actually watch a cricket play his tune. A little patience, a lot of time, a different view.

A routine miracle
December, 1990

The back door slammed shut, the wind pulling the knob out of my hand. Cold. Almost zero. It was late to be doing chores, 8:30. I could see the light in the barn. The eager baaing of the ewes expecting fresh hay and a sprinkling of grain echoed through the trees, the blackness of the night so close it seemed to cling like sticky tar. Without a moon, or much snow, the stars were no match for the dark. I shivered and looked up. Orion and Capella seemed farther away than ever, pinpricks in the vast sky.

The ground crunched under my feet. Trees moaned, then cracked like rifle shots. On a night like this, the outdoors becomes a threatening place. Usually the three rabbits scuttle across the barnyard in the dark, dancing like wraiths in the starlight. But on this night I saw no sign of ghostly long-eared creatures. They have a hole in the east side of the barn where they scoot into the hay bales. I imagined them there — gray beside black beside gray — huddled together for warmth.

The back of the barn is not lit. I entered, picking my way carefully between the John Deere with its alien arm, the back hoe, at rest like a monstrous appendage, and the ancient gray Ford, our neighbor Jack's friendly tractor. Its old engine makes a wonderful quaint sound in the July hayfields, steadfast and true.

A chicken flew, startled, from the Ford seat, and I jumped. But the murmur of my husband's voice as he talked to the sheep guided me into the heart of the barn. I closed up the chicken coop; the geese and the ducks quacked under their breath and rearranged themselves by the back door.

In the big center pen are three old Dorset ewes and their five lambs — all about a month old. They are calm and collected, old hands at lambing. I climbed into their pen to hug a few lambs who kicked and twisted, trying to escape my arms. But I cornered each one — Selma, Clara, Lulu, Henrietta, and an unnamed ram who has a bad eye — and gave them a Christmas pat. They still didn't care. Only their mothers pushed and shoved to get close to me because I might have grain. Few sheep have ever "loved" me for being me. They aren't like dogs.

We finished the chores, tarrying another moment to watch Lulu slip into the manger to eat from the top of the pile. It was then, when we were ready to come back to the house, that we thought we heard a tiny lamb's voice. We waited, listening, but only the wind answered. Just the same we took our flashlights, walked through the paddock and into the long stretch of fence which leads to the several-acre pasture that stretches from the forest to the front yard.

Again we heard the cry — distinct now and frequent, accompanied by the throaty nurturing answer of a ewe who has given birth. Unlike the usual uproar of hungry sheep's sounds, this ewe's voice was speaking to an offspring. When we found her in a grove of small saplings, there were two lambs, one white, one black. My husband scooped them up, and Midnight, the old ewe, followed. She has taken a liking to dropping her lambs in the pasture on stormy nights, but she is an old accomplished mother and both Magic and Mistletoe, the new lambs, had round bellies and were dry.

It seemed like a tiny miracle that above the howling wind we had heard the cry — that we had lingered in the barn longer than usual, and that in the darkness and acres of woods and fields we had found them at all.

Midnight and her lambs were bedded in the middle stall. My husband left me alone with them while he went to the house to mix the warm molasses water we give to new mothers. The peaceful spirit of a barn at night descended quickly. The disruption of new lambs gave way immediately to a resettling. Five roosters in the peak of the rafters fluffed and reseated themselves. The geese slipped their heads under their wings. The 35 ewes in the main paddock chewed and pulled mouthfuls of hay from the manger. Midnight stood quietly, nuzzling her lambs.

I started to pick up the grain bin area. One empty garbage can had two tiny, soft brown mice in the bottom of it, trapped. The mice had huge ears and long tails and wide eyes that were full of fear. I tipped the can over, and they scrambled as if I were a cat, running for shelter under the gate into the lambing pen. A barn is a wonderful place to be in winter in spite of the cold, for a special presence dwells within.

When Midnight finally got her molasses water, she drank quickly. We refilled the bucket, then flipped the light switch. Everything fell into darkness and silence except for the rhythmic breathing of animals. Seventy-six creatures sleep together in this place, never mind the seemingly limitless number of rodents and other weasel-related population that live under the hay bales and barn floors.

I walked back to the house swiftly. It was too cold to be out in the open for long. By morning, more lambs had arrived, two white ewes, one black ram. Then another white ram. That evening the barn was more abuzz than ever.

It is still cold out there, and on Christmas Eve now when I look back at the house from the paddock, the living room lights flicker in the spitting snow. The house is such a warm, cheery place with the woodstoves hot and hungry for logs, gobbling one after another. A kettle bubbles; someone pours a cup of tea. I am eager to get back inside.

But for a moment I hesitate. One more hug for a newborn lamb. One more scratch to an old ewe's ears. Then, guided by the tree near the little chicken coop, a tiny fir decorated with white lights that hold the promise of goodness, I follow the road back to the house and my family who waits inside. "Any new lambs?" they will ask.

"Not yet," is the reply. "But soon."

Celebrate as one
July, 1991

I have two favorite holidays and the Fourth of July is one of them. From the early morning wake-up when I scramble downstairs to fry (in the face of all healthy cooking warnings) doughnuts for the family, to the ending of the day, which is usually spent on the front porch with an array of children dancing like fairies across emerald grass and clutching silver sparklers in the fading twilight, I feel part of a truly magical midsummer celebration.

The day is special to me, not because I am a dyed-in-the-wool patriot, but because the Fourth of July exemplifies all that makes this country fascinating. It is the unhomogenized blending of all of us, as if we were put into a milk jar and yet the sterilization process refused to work. We remain who we are. Thomas Jefferson wrote that "all men are created equal... ." Literally, we are not equal, but in the eyes of a just government, we must be; one thing is clear, however, and that is we are different. It takes nothing more than a trip across this country to verify the variety. When the Fourth of July rolls around, we gather together in towns, villages, cities, on front porches, in back yards, at great ballparks, and oceanside beaches, in various shapes and forms — our unhomogenized way — to celebrate an idea.

It is within this idea, this celebration of a world-changing piece of paper that set the beginning of a new country in motion, that the Fourth of July arrived ten years ago in Big Timber, Montana — with a heart-stopping explosion at 7 a.m. We dashed to the front porch of our second story bunkhouse room and were greeted with the sight of nine riflemen's smoking guns, pointed toward the heavens, a salute to the bright, brilliant blue sky — and the Fourth.

Breakfast was not fresh doughnuts but mountain trout, caught in the pools of the fast-moving, icy-cold Sweet Grass River, a crystal clear swell of glacial melt from the Crazy Mountains which towered over the valley. We said our goodbyes after breakfast, one last bareback ride on Zach, a drink from the cold river, and loaded with camping gear we headed for Harlowton, an hour's drive north from the ranch.

Harlo, as the locals called the place, was as typical American West as one could ever find. There were no tourists. It was like being home in Bowdoinham, watching the preparations for the barbecue and the lineup for our parade where I would wave to friends and neighbors. Here, I wasn't a neighbor or friend, but somehow it seemed as if I were. The five of us stood in front of the Hotel Graves and waved to every float that passed by, from the Honey Queen to Smokey the Bear.

At noon the crowd headed to the local rodeo ring, a sight as common in western small towns as New England village greens are here. We had "reserved" seats in the south grandstand, which meant we were sitting with all the folks in the broiling sun. For the next four hours we hollered, waved our hats, drank the local beer, and roasted in the heat, while before our eyes cowboys and cowgirls rode saddle broncos, roped calves, raced each other through the barrel course, and wrestled steers. Little kids from the cheering crowd were chosen to ride sheep and yearlings, and we wondered if our lazy Maine sheep would tolerate a Fourth of July celebratory romp around an arena.

The bravest of all rode the Brahman bulls. The bulls' names echoed from the loud speaker's twangy voice, rolling like tumbleweed across the prairie and seemingly as innocuous — Rosebud, Smiley, Coors Lite, Mellow Yellow, and Sugarplum. Ah, yes. The thought of riding a bull named Sugarplum was almost beguiling.

It was a hot, smelly, sweaty, steamy Fourth. When we pulled out of Harlo at 5 p.m. we still had four hours of open road driving on Route 12 through land that is part of Montana without the spectacular western mountains. There were only sheep farms and lark buntings along this road. We pulled into Miles City for the night. It was odd, to be traveling by car when normally we'd be sitting on our porch watching the fireworks high above the city of Bath.

We checked into a motel that night, only $31 for all five of us, and ate at the local chuckburger place, 4 B's. From outside we could hear the report of fireworks. Our booth was next to a window, and in the fading twilight the celebration of this day was coming to a close. John Adams wanted the celebration of the Declaration of Independence to be "solemnized with pomp and parade, with shows, games, sports, guns, bells, bonfires, and illuminations, from one end of this continent to the other." It seemed as if we had done all those things, and we were at the other end of the continent — almost. The fireworks over Miles City, Montana, looked exactly like those in Bath, Maine. Sounded like them, too. Sparkled for the very same reason.

The next morning we were on the road at dawn. I drove through rough country now while the rest of the family slept. I saw seven deer and seven cars in two hours. Not one car was going in the same direction I was — east — into uninhabited land of North Dakota.

There are times like that when I think I could prowl the back roads of America for the rest of my days. Isolation is part of the appeal. Raw, stark nature is another part. But so is the experiencing of tiny American hamlets and cowtowns, villages, and small cities that each July will gather together to celebrate the idea that makes them one United States.

Lucky kitten
August, 1991

A skinny little imp is hiding in the front flower bed, crouched under the lovage plant, licking his chops and, if he is smart, thanking his lucky stars for this family that took him in, saving him from a heartless world. Surely, the unwary white-breasted nuthatch who has just flown into the feeder is uppermost on his mind. But if I were Harry, I would silently be celebrating the one year anniversary of my salvation.

An August afternoon last year, one of those hot and sticky days, found us wandering in the front yard, lazily inspecting coneflowers, counting how many bumblebees each flower head could support, and watching the antics of the fritillary butterflies. A catlike cry from the brambles at the edge of the creek attracted Jillian and Jake.

"Mom, a kitten."

"Nope," I replied, bird expert that I am. "Catbird."

"Mom." They were insistent.

I ignored them and kept on with my meanderings, snipping a petunia head off here, pulling a weed there, while the two of them plunged into the underbrush.

"You'll get poison ivy," I called after them.

They didn't. They got Harry instead.

Exceedingly small and fragile, the gray-black tabby huddled under the cinnamon ferns. His eyes were huge in an almost skeletal head. We brought him back to the house and offered milk which he lapped up immediately. Food followed. He gulped it down. We named him Little Cat, for in spite of my years of cat ownership (at one time in my childhood we "owned" 16 cats, 13 of whom were black), I had never seen anything so tiny without being supported by a mother. Little Cat huddled in the garage then, behind the recycling cans. We couldn't coax him out for the rest of the day.

I played the mother role, urging the kids to stay away. "You don't know what diseases he might have." So Harry, a.k.a. Little Cat, spent the night outdoors, again. He slept curled up on a pickup truck box which was next to the front steps. The next morning we coaxed and cajoled again, fed him, and generally watched him hide. By that evening I had relented and he slept inside, locked in the bathroom.

He stayed there for a few more nights; after he broke a pot of flowers on the windowsill, I moved him to the laundry room. All the while I kept promising to call the Humane Society while my young son called every single person he knew. "We have this cute little cat that we found and were wondering…" Their answers were just like ours. Like everyone else, we already owned cats — two calicos who were very set in their ways. Immediately Huckleberry Pie unequivocally put her foot down. No new kittens. She is the weasel killer in the family, and it was all we could do to keep her from creaming Little Cat. Pippin followed an ignore-it-and-he'll-go-away attitude. But the meaning of her low, threatening growl was obvious. I could not imagine having three fighting cats in the house every day. Besides, Little Cat didn't stand a chance. He had to go.

Yet the August days ticked by and we became more complacent about this spit of a kitten who wandered around my feet. We took him to the vet's. "At least," I said, "he will be healthy and have his first shots for his next home."

Our vet found Little Cat to be infested with fleas and ear mites. "I am sure he has shared these with your other cats," Sue said with a sympathetic smile. It had been a season for dropped-off animals, and it was becoming a bit wearing in the veterinarian's office.

Little Cat came home, complete with a computer printout of his medical history, a made-up birth date, and a heavy dose of ear mite medicine. The other cats, who had to suffer through the ear drops, too, loved him even less.

Actually none of us really loved him, but we had become attached enough to change his name to Harry — Harold when we were really cross. The amazing thing about this whole ordeal was that I was never really cross. Other than the original broken vase, Harry had never wet the floor, scratched a carpet, broken a dish or even leaped on a table. (A year later things have changed, but not much. He still remains one of the best-behaved cats I have ever had.)

We were all weakening. My son could find no prospective owners. We knew his fate at the Humane Society was uncertain. My sister is a vet and has tales of unwanted animals. Although she lives in Indiana, I know things are no different here in Maine. "Animal ownership is not a right," she says. "It is a responsibility."

Those thoughts echoed in my mind. Did I want one more animal responsibility? However, the clincher came about the end of the third week. We also have in this household a much-maligned golden retriever named Casey. The two calico cats hate Casey, and she fears them, cowering whenever they enter a room.

The humans in this family love Casey — sort of. She has bad habits like eating disgusting stuff. She has a chronic skin condition that makes her smelly when wet, which is most of the time. So none of us holds her or hugs her for hours on end. But Harry changed all that — and by doing so insured a comfortable future for himself.

Harry loves Casey. Once he was let out of the laundry room at night, unlike the other cats, he did not venture upstairs to sleep on our bed. Instead, this little two-pound wonder crawled onto Casey's green plaid dog pillow and slept tucked under the chin of a mangy old dog. Every morning we would find Casey and Harry, friends indeed, snuggled together in the sunlight.

They have tussle times together, too. Like the lion tamer in the circus, Harry will put his head completely inside Casey's mouth. Then, scrambling with his back paws, he tries frantically to escape while Casey smiles and thumps her tail on the floor. Or Harry will bite Casey all over the head. Casey bites back. Harry flips over to the top of Casey's head, straddling her ears, then dances back and the romp starts all over again. Rejects themselves, they have found a place.

A year has passed. Harry is still very small, weighing not much over five pounds. He spent the winter evenings on top of the kitchen cabinets just under the ceiling. The other cats still make life miserable for him, but his agility allows him to escape easily. He is even brave enough now to tease them just a little. He has spent the summer stalking birds, much to my frustration. So there are times, like when the bluebirds fledged, that he has had to stay inside for days on end.

He wasn't happy, but "Such is life, Harry," I say to him.

Actually, such is life for him. We all love him now, except perhaps the mole he brought home this morning. His yellow-green eyes shine with mischief and good health. He doesn't purr much, but he does crawl onto our laps in the evening and snuggle down, rearranging himself into a tiny ball. I suppose that under that lovage plant right now, while he contemplates another bird, he is celebrating his year of care at our hands and his friendship with a dog. He's been lucky.

Making hay
September, 1991

I never made hay until I was a grown woman. In spite of 18 years spent living surrounded by Indiana farmers and their fields, with rows of soybeans within feet of my back yard swing and oats so close to my bedroom window that itchy black oatbugs would crawl through my screens at night, I had never made hay. Occasionally, I would watch Mr. Schlaudroff's machinery scooping up wheat stalks and spitting out bales of straw. But somehow, I missed out on the real adventure.

Then came the years long after I had moved to Maine, when my older son Arek was 11, 12, 15. A friend who worked the oceanside meadows near our home took this young man under his wing and taught him the art of farming. In the neat, orderly rows that lay like a quilter's thread across a blanket, the boy saw beauty and wonder. He learned how to hay, and — translating those bits of alfalfa and clover and goldenrod onto paper — how to draw.

Now, he is grown and like yesterday's chaff, the wind has taken him to other places, where he draws landscapes for a living. But there is a legacy left here for us, one that the two younger children have taken over. Haying is now a family affair, and although I play the bit actor's part in the whole event, I still feel a connection to this process of putting by a field's bounty.

Somewhere tucked in the deep recesses of the human heart, most of us find a nostalgic tug that pulls, even stretches us to reach for that almost-lost way of life. Foremost among trends for the 21st century is the fact that the majority of Americans will live in cities, yet only one out of four people will actually be glad to be there. The rest of us will strive to recapture home through magazines and vacations that resemble the good old days. Perhaps I am already feeling some of that connection. Like a spider's web that refuses to break in spite of the wind and rain, I want to keep these bonds strong that tie us to the land.

Late last month at dark when the fireflies came out, I was standing alone on the back deck, thinking. There was movement in the barn. A flashlight winked through the darkness, like the lightning bugs, blinking its friendly greeting to me. My husband was covering the last of the day's bales, tucking them in to protect them from night time dew. When Arek was home, we were never this late in bringing in the bales. The haying was done on a schedule. Now it is done catch as catch can. But still with good spirits.

Earlier that day, when the grass was deemed just right, the crew had set out, water jug, heavy gloves, bandanas, and sun tan cream packed in the back of the old Ford, which has served for many years as a receptacle for the junk used in haying; things like baling twine, grease, tools, gasoline cans, funnels, and baseball caps are essential ingredients. It is all there in the truck — and it seems to stay there from season to season. In the middle of winter I can always find the August bug spray.

Jillian now is in charge of raking. She hasn't mastered the corners yet, but she is quick and efficient, and the rows come out serviceable, if not beautiful. Jacob runs the baler. At 13 he is picking up where his older brother Arek left off. A connection has been made, and the farming baton is passed. He may have a few more mishaps than someone more experienced, but with time that will change. The back of the hay wagon has been cracked where he hit a pine tree. And once, while looking backward to see what sort of progress he was making, his forward movement was stopped abruptly when he hooked the corner of the tractor on another huge pine tree. But he, too, is a willing worker and seems to delight in the sense of outdoor adventure and accomplishment.

Picking up and stacking bales is the difficult part for us. We have lost the strength and power in the family. This year it has been supplemented with volunteer contributions from a neighbor Hal who brings his little son and daughter to watch. With the energy of young people and hired hands from another neighbor boy Brandon, we have been able to pile the bales into the barn. They may not be as well-stacked, nor as equally balanced as in years gone by, but still, we say, it smells good. The bales settle down with a certain sense of satisfaction, a smugness to their nestling into nooks and corners of the barn, as if to say, this is indeed where we belong. We hold in our stems the summer's sunshine, a little bit of the earth's bounty, and here we will wait to be used.

And then there was a surprise this year. Labor Day arrived, and with the holiday our older son came home for the weekend. We made hay. He set out almost immediately the next morning to cut and then to ted the following day, announcing that the temperature and winds were just right to bale Monday afternoon.

There is always a sense of anxiety on Labor Day afternoon for most of us in this household — what will the first day of school be like? Do I have all my lessons complete? Will I like my teachers? Will I like my students? Do I have everything I need for college? Did I pack too many sweaters for Virginia? The answers vary and won't be found until Tuesday when some of us leave home for far away places and others begin the routine of the school year.

So now while it was Monday still, we all decided to leave those questions hanging at home. Hopping into the old truck, we headed two miles down the road to the waiting field. My husband did the corny, touristy thing — he brought the video camera. We all harassed him, accusing him of being trendy. We didn't want our pictures taken. But he ignored our jibes, saying, "When I am old and it is winter, I am going to sit and watch my family make hay on the video screen." Our sneers subsided. We actually climbed into the wagon and saluted.

He captured it all: our daughter driving the 4-cylinder Ford that every year our neighbor loans us ("It's good for the old machine," Jack says); our younger son in his seat on the John Deere, operating the baler, our older son with the strength of youth stacking bales onto the wagon, and me riding on top of everything, waving to my husband.

A motherless lamb
January, 1992

The voice of hunger is calling from the kitchen. Tilly, the orphan lamb, is making life complicated around here, requiring feedings every four hours, bed cleaning each evening, and mopping of the floor after one of her frolics. Tilly, in fact, has gotten in the way of everything.

But there is a fun side to all of this, too. Like the newborn year, Tilly has brought freshness to the day. She is like a soft January snowflake, twirling its way downward and being tossed up again by a gust of wind. Tilly twirls and spins, flops — and then leaps to her feet.

She is 13 days old today, and as I fix her bottle, her constant baaing and pestering remind me of the urgency of new life. She was motherless and premature, and for the first few days, we gave her little chance of living. She couldn't suckle well. Like a rag doll her head would flop from one side to the other. Every four hours around the clock, we fed her, nuzzled her, pretended as best we could to be sheep ourselves. Our friend Dian came to stay the New Year's Eve night, and soon she, too, was nuzzling and encouraging Tilly to drink. "Come on Tilly" was the battle cry.

Tilly's tiny face, scrunched-up eyes, and soft tongue contributed to our need for her to live. "You just have to," we would whisper in her ear. It is a funny thing, trying to will an animal to live. I want to believe so hard that this creature will survive. I play at being superhuman, beaming strength from my body into hers, yet at every 2 a.m. feeding I would approach her box with trepidation, fearing for certain that I would find only an inert little body. To dispel this fear, the very first night I slept with her. It has worked before. It worked this time.

As each day passed, Tilly gained in strength, and shortly after New Year's Day we reached the milestone where we could sleep through the night, feeding her late and very early. She still slept the entire time between feedings; often we had to wake her to remind her it was time to eat. But by five days she had increased her intake of milk and was actually attempting to walk. She had difficulty controlling all four legs at once, but when she finally ventured off the blanket where we usually fed her and started to nuzzle and suck on the strings of an apron hanging by the stove, there was cause for celebration in the household.

The next big step came the morning when my husband, shivering against the cold after the barn chores, found her standing up, bright-eyed and bushy-tailed, in her box. She was ready for breakfast. The following day she leaped out of the box, like a sheep being counted in a dream, and whatever semblance of peace that was left in the kitchen vanished with her flight. From the far corners of the attic, we extracted a metal dog kennel. With a lock on the door and bars all around, we would at least be able to "house" Tilly when we needed, in a lamb playpen.

That is where she is these days. Each night we change her blanket and cover it with fresh hay. She doesn't like being caged and protests loudly about it. The reasons are obvious. She has discovered the world. The wood pile is great for climbing into and chewing; the golden retriever and her bed are even greater sources of joy and entertainment. The dog's collar acts as a pacifier for Tilly. And the dog is patient enough to sit quietly while Tilly sucks on her collar. Then there is the runway, a perfect circle that passes through the kitchen, hallway, dining room, and den and back to the kitchen. She and the dog run like crazy to raise a ruckus when Tilly feels bored. Or she stands under the table and pretends she is in a barn, with the table cloth, like hanging fleece, and chair legs like a flock of sheep.

Of course, she has no idea what a real barn is like. We brought another lamb in to visit her once, but she ignored him. When she finally moves to the barn, sadly, she too, will be ignored. She won't have a bond. Her ties will always be with us. She relies on us to survive.

After I feed her this morning, she and I will go for a romp. We've introduced her to the bustling, brimming-over world of the outdoors. At first she shivered and stayed right at my heels, crying piteously. Days later, she had become adventurous enough to chase the flock of chickens. Other creatures fascinate her. She waits for the cats to come in the door, eyeing them speculatively, before she trots out.

Lamb-hopping is her favorite activity. She learned it in the kitchen where she would practice her second base slides — run, hop, slide into the base sequence — but she has perfected it outside. Up and down the driveway we run. With a little encouragement from me, she's become an expert. My hops are passable, but wouldn't win a prize at any sheep show. Tilly doesn't seem to mind. She's making out just fine with what she's got.

Squirrels always win
February, 1992

When winter days hang on endlessly, like a lingering cold, and temperatures can never make up their minds whether to try minus four degrees or plus eight, I plop into a chair and do nothing for a while but stare out the window. In this trancelike state I realize that what I am actually doing is watching gray squirrels —rodents, of all things — for entertainment.

I don't want to believe that days have become such a string of white and cold that only *Sciurus carolinensis* relieves the monotony. Perhaps, I say to myself, it's not just these gray fluffy creatures who look as if they have just returned from a wash and blow dry at the local beauty salon, but the tantalizing aspects of lovely jewel-like birds at the feeders which attracts me to the window. At least I'd like to think that it is the birds who are the attraction. The spirit of winter personified in chickadees arrives in droves. Everywhere, constantly, all day long, the sprites of the forest bark their hoarse call, "Chick-a-dee-dee," as they swoop with the grace of an Olympic athlete into the feeding platform. Yes, they are the reason I sit and stare, I reassure myself.

And if chickadees are not the reason I watch the feeder, surely the flock of 30 goldfinches, with manners polite and colors dull, like evening grosbeaks who have endured a shrink cycle in a hot dryer, are the attraction; they are so — well — sweet. Daily, too, are the visits from downy and hairy woodpeckers who eat as much sunflower seeds as they do suet; this is intriguing behavior. Today when I balanced precariously in my bathrobe and L.L. Bean boots, filling the highest feeder from the top rung of my step ladder, a female downy did not move, but clung to the other side of the feeder house while I dumped in the sunflowers.

And if chickadees, goldfinches, and woodpeckers are not the reason I stare at feeders, clearly the antics of white-breasted nuthatches who scamper and poke, believing that each tree crevice will hold a treasure (or even the raucous behavior of the blue jays) are the real delight. But I am only deluding myself. There are none at the feeders who bring as many howls of laughter and cries of frustration as the gray squirrels who have moved in with all their kin for this winter's duration.

At first only one or two of them fed daily. These were easily tolerated. There are five different feeders hanging from the apple trees so there was always enough space for birds and squirrels alike. But one day, relatives started appearing — relatives that human in-laws would prefer not to claim — the kind who eat all the beer and pretzels, burp and leave their mess behind. Squirrels, however, seem to be unoffended by greed and slovenliness. In fact, those with a few manners left just modeled themselves after the old uncle. The squirrel gene for politeness, long lost, has been replaced by one that breeds gluttony. At a population of 20 squirrels per acre, I figure we could be in for an attack in the thousands. Like hoards of Huns crossing the Volga, the starving squirrels invade.

So frustrating had this Hun-like behavior become, that once the original responses on our part — screaming, pounding on the window (the squirrels soon realized that noise does not harm), hucking apples (I would never make the Atlanta Braves), flapping nightclothes (one squirrel actually seemed to be fascinated by pink flannel), running barefoot into the snow with raised sword (broom) in hand — ceased to work, we got serious. Out came the BB gun. It was fired several times. Now we have one cracked pane of glass in the kitchen where the BB, which of course missed the squirrel, ricocheted off the tree and careened into the window.

It was after the window-smashing episode that my husband took over the shooting task. He was a success, killing four squirrels in five minutes. The others scattered rather quickly at the beginning of the rampage and actually had the decency and respect for their departed brothers to not return for forty-five minutes. The bodies lay there for a week, to my husband's thinking, as signals to the little buggers, but the squirrels just climbed over them and continued to chow down on black oil sunflower seeds. As an aside, hunters kill over 40 million squirrels yearly in the eastern United States; that doesn't dent the population.

So, we did what normal humans do. We bought a book , written by another human, Bill Adler, on squirrels. *Outwitting Squirrels* is the actual title. I found it in mint condition in a used book store. That should have been a clue.

The book includes sections like "Know the Enemy, Over-the-Counter Anti-Squirrel Structures and Devices, 101 Cunning Stratagems, What to do if you Think Squirrels are Cute." There's also an appendix called "Resources." We needed them.

Following the book's advice, we have tried all the standards — hanging feeders (our squirrels, like everyone's, are expert circus performers and can walk any tightrope, eat in any position, all without a safety net), spinning satellite feeders (squirrels just hang on and get dizzy while they eat — probably some sort of a natural high). We made teeny-tiny feeders out of plastic peanut butter jars, with only one small chickadee sized hole at the bottom (that feeder now has several large holes and is held together by duct tape). We set out decoy feeders (we paid $2.97 for ten ears of field corn which the blue jays ate), and we put lights in the trees (the squirrels chewed all the connections in half and not one was electrocuted — last spring we found three Christmas tree bulbs, red, blue, and green, at the edge of the woods some fifty feet from the feeder).

Arek is now urging us to try Nixalite, four feet long stainless steel strips with

120 needle-sharp points radiating from the metal. This stuff, which can be bent to cover any feeder that we wish to protect from squirrels, looks like barbed wire with three inch spikes. I am certain the front yard would take on the appearance of a war zone. But then, maybe that is what my Huns-in-the-disguise-of-squirrels might expect. The book warns that once Nixalite appears, Mr. Nice Rodent is gone.

I just know that we are smarter and stronger than squirrels. Hopefully, we can win. That's why I'm sitting at the kitchen table this morning watching seven pathetic chickadees wait for a scrap of seed tossed as a handout from the eleven squirrels who now control all the feeders.

Ravens
April, 1992

Ravens — those dark, haunting birds of night, remote northern forests, and Edgar Allen Poe — are doing their unusual, or better said in this neck of the woods, their usual thing. They've arrived with the month of April and are now content to spend their early morning hours close to human habitation. Both of them are coming as regularly as clockwork to the sheep's paddock some time shortly after 6 a.m. "Breakfast is served," a distant voice of the forest has announced. And breakfast this year consists of raw goose eggs on the half shell, served on the upper floor of the barn to two gleaming, glossy black birds.

Last year during the month of April the ravens would arrive daily. Their landing pattern evolved when they materialized out of nowhere and were suddenly seen circling over the fenced area to the south of the barn. They banked sharply, swooping through the pines that stand below the pasture and came in on a low, direct line to the north. This approach allowed for a smooth landing, either on the back of a sleeping ewe or on the half boards on the south side of the barn. The barn itself is a pole barn with one entire side exposed to sun and weather — and, as it seems now, to raven arrivals as well. A four foot high fence keeps the sheep inside. Anything that flies or is small and scurries can easily gain access to the barn.

When we first noticed these marauders, they were jumping up and down on our placid ewes, like kids on a trampoline, pulling fleece from the backs of the sheep, and then absconding with mouthfuls of wool, presumably to warm their nest. The sheep ignored them or looked at them with a bored yawn, treating the ravens' pecking like a cow treats a fly. The ravens continued to pick and poke around the barn yard, too, snatching up discarded bits of string and old fleece. Hay was also a favorite; frequently we would spot one as it flew away, looking like an inky Santa Claus with fleece and hay sticking out of both sides of its beak and hanging down the front like a beard.

When the ravens disappeared into the barn, we would stand at the living room window and wait about a minute before they reappeared, flapping their wings to gain altitude, heading south, but soon banking toward the west — the interior of this forested land and the site of their nest. We knew nothing of their in-barn behavior until one early morning when Pete was quietly at work at the north entrance to the barn. He caught the villains in the act. One raven glided in and, without a moment's hesitation, jumped up to a hen's nest in the hay mow, snatched an egg, cracked it open, and slurped down the contents. The raven paid little attention to the human standing nearby. Now these bums were getting serious. Stealing fleece and hay was one thing; eating our eggs was another.

Things got worse. The ducklings hatched and one by one six little yellow balls of fluff were scarfed down. We tried penning the ducks, but without success, and so the duckling population was depleted — and finally annihilated. It was a bit discouraging, but still the ravens and their clever antics were a surprising twist to barn life, and we were fascinated by them.

I went to the library that summer and read the newest book on ravens, a research of those in northern Vermont. Indeed, these birds were full of surprises and unexpected intelligent behavior, and our experiences were confirming that.

With the arrival of a new April, the ravens appeared on the paddock fence right on schedule. Like harbingers of light and spring instead of bearers of darkness and winter nights, the two coughed out their raucous greeting to the morning sunshine and slipped into the barn with the grace of ballet dancers.

Inside, with eyes keen on finding this spring's meals, they discovered the goose nest. These eggs, numbering 12 or 15, provided breakfast for two weeks. Each morning we would watch as a raven retreated from the paddock with a large white egg shell in its beak. Each day we checked the nest with its decreasing egg supply.

Actually, we don't really mind that the goose nest is gone. Those silly creatures have never successfully raised goslings in over ten years, but they spend a lot of time squawking about it. We're just as glad the ravens have tidied up the barn a little ahead of our spring-cleaning schedule.

Forest intrigue
October, 1992

The forest in October blazes like a raging wildfire, out of control, determined in its color and light changes to sweep the earth clean of any remaining green. This kind of forest fire attracts, unlike the real thing, enticing the wanderer into the far reaches of its secrets, guarded by flaming maples, dashing ash and birch, and somber oaks. The pathway into the hidden recesses, once lined with the gentle greens of ladyferns and goldthread, is covered now with wet, slick, decaying leaves. The brittle remains of cinnamon ferns look like their name. Bittersweet, twining its way through the blackberry patch, reaches out and snags the feet of the unwary traveler, its orange berries mocking each stumbling misstep.

The autumn forest intrigues, but, with color spread like an inviting banquet, it does not threaten. And yet there is a sharpness, a tension in the air. An October forest is not filled with the softness of an awakening woods in May, one alive with the red and white of trillium and the chartreuse of a chestnut-sided warbler.

So it is in October that I venture toward forest walks with a heightened sense of anticipation. That eager anticipation was part of autumn in Indiana. Trees were few and far between where I lived, so a trip to my grandparents in southeastern Ohio's hill country was the highlight of October when I was little. My brothers Jack and Jim and sister Jill and I would spend the weekend with endless relatives — cousins of my mother whom I saw only once a year, my aunt and uncle, my grandparents and their friends, our new playmates — and in that tiny Ohio town, population 100, we would gather together to explore the wooded hills in search of bittersweet.

We matched the colors of the trees in our flannel plaid jackets and head scarves. It was not a time of Patagonia colors like jade and fuchsia. Then we wore red and black, orange and brown, and my grandmother looked as lovely as the trees she passed under.

In those days the hickories and yellow poplars around their cabin had not grown tall, and so we had a view across the valley where Holstein cows grazed under the shade of orange maples. We always came home from that autumn weekend having jumped in leaf piles for hours on end, clutching armfuls of bittersweet to decorate the house for Thanksgiving. There was no electricity or running water at the cabin, and life was simple for a child at play in the woods.

Years later, when my children were small and autumn approached, we would travel down the road near our small Maine farm to a heavily wooded and then largely unpopulated area, where there was an extensive swamp, surrounded by alders and aging pines. We pretended that a witch lived there, one we called Fifinella after a witch in a children's book. As the days shortened and darkness came earlier, as winds howled and leaves swirled to the ground making hissing sounds, Fifinella's swamp became the perfect forest to scare us as much as we wanted.

The road to the swamp was a washboard and the truck jerked and jolted us as we approached. "Who made these leaves such a brilliant color?" we would wonder. One who used a lunatic's palette of spectacular hues. Only a witch. The swamp's bottom was thick with ooze, yet the water was clear enough to act like a black mirror, catching and holding forever the reflection of anyone who dared peer into the water. A midnight mirror. We drove home the long way on October nights, just to go through the forest and past Fifinella's Swamp, to shiver and shudder when we heard her laughter ring with the cry of the wind through the falling leaves.

But the forest can be a combination of excitement and gentle wonders at the same time, like my grandparents' forest and Fifinella's Swamp in one. Last week we joined our dear friends Jane and Phil and hiked many miles to a mountain peak, caught by an early autumn gale, with winds so strong on the top that it was difficult to stand upright. Fog shrouded the mountain and we saw only the white tapestry around it. Our imaginations had to paint the dragon-flame orange, blood-red, and fire-yellow of maples on the canvas. Along the trail we saw the first signs of winter hibernation — recent bear scat filled with the seeds of berries. Some time, not so much earlier than our passage, one of those heavy black creatures had lumbered over the same path we were taking.

We hiked for the entire day — up and down — and then my husband and I returned at dusk to the foot of the mountain where a lodge stood, stark and strong, invitingly lit in the evening mist. Pete and I, however, were going a mile back up the mountain to a cabin without electricity. As we started up the woods road, a smoke-gray cat sprinted from a thicket, meowed once, and proceeded to follow us up the trail. It was raining steadily and the cat was as wet as we were. Although each passing minute brought increasing darkness and more rain, the cat did not turn back to the warmth and security of the lodge. She pushed on with us, brushing against grasses that at times obliterated her from our view. Who was this creature, seemingly so comfortable in the hidden corners of the forest? Had we been near Fifinella's Swamp, I would have looked over my shoulder.

The darkness increased, obscuring the tops of the menacing trees. The dying goldenrod and asters writhed like spirits along the path. We were unable to be sure of the trail that would lead us to the cabin. As if sensing our insecurity, the cat — this cat of copse and wilderness — took the lead, and soon we three arrived on the porch.

The cabin itself was nestled in a stand of maple, ash, and pine, towering trees that dwarfed our sleeping site. Our friends were inside with the woodstove blazing, Jane's chili bubbling on it, and the lanterns glowing. We marched in, with our new companion, the snowshoe-pawed cat, who seemed unafraid of the secrets the forest kept hidden. The cat spent the evening, eating chili, drying herself in a comfortable lap, dozing on the foot of a sleeping bag, until at midnight she awoke us with her mouse-chasing antics. We let her out. She disappeared into the deep darkness of the night, swallowed up like just another mystery kept by an October forest.

BOOK III: VISITORS

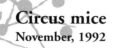

Circus mice
November, 1992

The wheelbarrow was old, covered with a piece of gray, splintered plywood. It reminded me of one of November's discarded apples, wormy, rotten, rust-colored, useless. Jake's intent was just to clean up the place, get the wheelbarrow out of sight, but when he actually began the process, moving the wheelbarrow at a lumbering pace along the driveway, lump-lumping on its single flat tire, a traveling circus exploded. Mice scurried everywhere, leaping from holes at the base of the barrow itself, scrambling up over the edges, slipping beneath the plywood, and tumbling off the front wheel brace where one unfortunate fellow was immediately run over.

Actually all of this activity was performed by only three mice, but frantic rodents have the ability to create the illusion of mass and, therefore, multitudes in confusion. Cautiously, so as not to create another chaotic fire drill, Jake lifted the plywood cover and peeked inside. A nest of grasses, milkweed down, and dry oak leaves woven together like a piece of finest cloth was tucked in the corner of the barrow, the home of white-footed mice.

When Jake stopped the forward movement, one mother-type mouse huddled by the side of the driveway, peering out from behind a cluster of field pussytoes. She refused to disappear. Her young was stranded, squeaking in distress from the wheelbarrow. With dark eyes sprinkled with fear, incessantly twitching whiskers and nose, this young mouse began to play "hide and escape" on the braces of the wheelbarrow. First, he was on the wheel. Swish! He was clinging to the inside of the handle. Zing! He was perched on the cross beam support.

Jake and I (he had appealed for my help, "Moooom!") were caught in this tiny drama. What to do? Disrupting mice seemed insignificant, yet, when faced with the actual courage of these tiny, ubiquitous creatures, it was not so easy to dismiss their plight.

The obvious first move was to put the plywood lid back on the wheelbarrow and leave the scene, hoping that nature would take its course and allow the mice family (minus one) to regroup. We did that. An hour later, the mother was gone, but the baby remained, clinging to the braces of the wheel. Now we felt even more responsible for having destroyed the family unit. And we had to get the wheelbarrow out of the middle of the driveway. Thus began a slow-paced push toward the chicken coop. Jake provided the power; I crawled along on all fours keeping a careful eye on the white-footed mouse suspended precariously above the driveway.

Once behind the coop, we coaxed and prodded the tiny creature until it slipped inside the barrow itself, where it sat a moment beside the nest, its sides moving in and out rapidly, looking like a miniature bellows at work. We added two apples, a handful of sheep's fleece, and a pile of black oil sunflower seeds, grabbed our calico cats and relegated them to the kitchen, and left the scene, keeping our fingers crossed.

For a day we did nothing. Then we peeked again. To our somewhat silly delight, we discovered a rather large heap of opened hulls from the sunflower seeds. The apple had nibbles taken from it. Within two more days the seeds were all shelled, and I found myself leaving another small hoard when I fed the birds. This was getting ridiculous.

And it has gotten more so. My evening routine has altered a bit — off to the garden to pick parsley for the rabbits, back to the hutches to feed Sparky and Pignut, the two caged rabbits, and Wally, Sticky-Bun and Crow, the three rabbits that run free, to the coop to grain the 25 bantams, and now this added side trip. Behind the coop, tucked in-between two ash trees is the red canoe. There are several bales of old hay nearby and a pile of cut logs beneath the canoe, all prospective sites for a new mouse house. The wheelbarrow is next to the canoe. I lift the plywood, dump in another handful of sunflower seeds to add to the cache and take stock of the situation.

Things are quiet in the woods now while the trees, dark sentinels, await the first snow. The wheelbarrow appears empty, the mouse nest a bit flattened and dispirited. But at some time there has been activity about. These seeds are shelled by some creature in the dark. Our mouse is here, somewhere, I just know it.

I allow myself to feel a little better. Yet soon the November winds will increase, shoving the first real storm of the season upon us. Like a spitting cat, the sleet-snow will pounce upon the earth, creating enough commotion to scare the most daring mice. We have a little, lonely one to look after. Jake and I will tend him through this winter.

Escape to the barn
December, 1992

I went out to the barn this afternoon when it wasn't time to do the chores. If the clouds hadn't been piled, one gray pillow on top of the other, I could have seen the sun hanging just above the tree line. I slipped over the fence on the east side of the paddock to avoid the geese and their incessant honking. I wanted peace. In the barn, Sam the ram peered through his fence, but he keeps quiet these days. I silently crossed the frozen earth, pockmarked with hundreds of cloven hoof indentations. What was once November mud is now December hardpan.

On the west side of the barn is the newly-opened section of the paddock.

Here a giant hemlock tree, hanging heavy with tiny cones like Christmas ornaments, stands like a protective umbrella in the center of the area. A small creek, essentially empty with but a trickle of water clinging to the bottom like shards of glass, meanders at an angle toward the obscured setting sun. The sheep seem to like this patch of land away from a direct view into the barn.

Ours is an open south-facing structure which allows plenty of sunlight to enter the barn in winter. If you are a sheep who has to be enclosed, you like this. But if you are an outside sheep looking in, it can be a noisy, bothersome place full of crowing roosters, cackling hens, and honking geese.

This afternoon there are twenty-three ewes outside, sixteen of whom should be pregnant. Number 19 looks ready to deliver any minute. She is built like a tank, slung low to the ground and, when she spies me, gets to her feet looking a bit like my father does when disturbed from a quiet afternoon in front of the football game. Once Number 19 is up, the others, who are scattered on the ground like moguls on a ski slope, get to their feet, too, their ears cocked forward with an air of surprise. No one comes to the barn at this hour of the day.

I just read a farm book in which the author explores the idea that sheep are not really dumb creatures at all; rather, their annoying habits, like running en masse right through fences, are logical responses to situations. Sheep have no defenses. They have no way to fight except by flight. I could see that look about them now. Until they were sure who had arrived in their paddock, they needed to be prepared to escape.

For a moment I have become a tomten making my rounds of the farm animals on Christmas night. I whisper to them, "Sheep, fat ewes, stay warm in your wool coats — eat your alfalfa hay." I repeat the mantra. Who am I to know whether these words work for soothing sheep on a December evening or not?

I crouch against the fence post and call Tilly's name. A small, thickly-fleeced ewe separates herself from the group. She trots over to me. Down low is the best level for greeting Tilly; she likes to nuzzle in close and then get her nose and chin scratched. My husband calls her annoying, but I can easily call her lovable. Tilly stays with me, and I am glad, for I have decided to stay with the sheep for a long time. It is hectic in the house. We are cleaning for the holidays and everyone is helping. I have no complaints, but still…

An old friend whom we had not seen for twenty years came for coffee this morning. With him arrived a flood of memories. Wasn't it only yesterday that we were young? I ask Tilly about time flying and holiday meanings and such; her response is to push closer, snuffling for a handful of grain and another hug — the simple needs.

The barn is the place to go during the holiday season. And the sheep are the animals from whom I seek comfort. They don't wag their tails like our dog in blind affection nor are they as cozy and intimate as the cats. Sheep are accepting, tolerant, non-demanding. I expect to sit here for half an hour, talking out loud to them. They will listen without comment.

Teeny Spot, who looks like she ran into a wall and was squashed from both ends, comes nearer to see what is up with Tilly. Tilly is, of course, the tamest, and the others stand watching her behavior with a human, but I suspect Teeny Spot wants to know a little more about me. Maybe before winter is over I will know more about her. She is the great grandchild of my first ewe, Cassie, and by that bloodline alone captures a corner of my heart.

Leaning against the fence, not moving for a long time, I can feel the temperature dropping. The air is ice-cracking cold. Snow swirls furiously in fragments of ice chips. I feel like I am part of a scene from one of those magical Christmas globes which some giant's child has just picked up and given a shake. Here I am, caught in the "barn and shepherd scene," just right for Christmas.

It grows darker. A few older ewes are no longer curious about my voice or my ideas and they turn away, walking in their slightly stiff-legged manner, looking for all the world like matrons on the streets of Pittsburgh or Chicago, finishing the holiday shopping in their thick fur coats. These matrons, however, are content to wander back to the welcoming shelter of the hemlock boughs and have no interest in Marshall Field's windows.

I stretch my legs. All the sheep except Tilly move away now. Tilly is still intent on grain. She knows I have a handful of cracked corn waiting somewhere. We walk together back to the barn and I produce her treat. She snuffles, inhaling the kernels from the palm of my blue mitten. I scratch her head one more time before I return to the lighted house. Electric candles have been turned on in the windows, inviting the traveler, the friend, the adult-child coming home, or the shepherd to come inside and stay a while.

An hour in the company of sheep was all I needed. They reminded me what should be done during December.

Contented and nowhere else to be
July, 1993

Given the present human condition caught between an out-of-control deficit and a severely threatened environment — let alone day to day worries — it is a wonder that any of us find a moment of peace or serenity.

Take right now, for instance. I am sitting in the sun on the back porch watching three white geese nip off pieces of grass as they wander along the bank of the tiny creek, where purple violets and sensitive fern grow. The geese edge away from the stream to a spot where the grass is greener and eat, the sound a bit like that of humans chewing lettuce — crisp. Occasionally, one goose will speak to another, a throaty murmur. And so the afternoon goes on; the sun shines; the breeze blows. If I concentrate on watching the geese and only think about these three, their peaceful pursuit slips into my day. But, if I am not careful, the concerns of tomorrow, of deadlines to meet and projects to complete, soon creep back. Contentment is elusive.

In the front yard a cat seems, like the geese, to have captured a slice of contentment for the day. Huckle, our very deceptive calico, lies in the sun between the lovage and columbine plants, her paws resting like a sphinx. Her tail switches on occasion, seeming to belie her casual attitude about the day. The bird feeder hanging five feet above her head is alive with purple finches and rose-breasted grosbeaks. Behind her, and eight feet higher, two bluebirds inspect and reinspect the bird house. Indeed, Huckle may be in some kind of cat heaven.

She is a most unusual cat — a non-meowing, softly purring, perfectly proper lady. Immaculate to a fault. Prissy to the point of irritation. Her white is always white; her honey-colors are never mussed; her black is sprinkled with gray which creates the softening effect of a gentle cat — which she is not. Instead with Huckle, you get a lie. Underneath the proper behavior lives a terror. She beheads weasels and systematically kills red squirrels.

Given her personality, I could wonder if she ever has a sense of contentment. But something about her approach this day tells me, and apparently the birds as well, that she isn't a threat at the moment. Her tail may have been unable to resist a few warning twitches, but her overall demeanor indicates satisfaction with the day as it is. As the afternoon wears on, that proves to be true. Even those of us with temperaments of fire find moments in time when everything is just as it should be.

Every once in a while, a summer's day comes along when I don't know the date, when I have no place to go, and the phone never rings. Sometimes it happens on the farm — it did the first day of summer last year. My journal entry reads "Jacob and I spent the first day of summer in the pond." That's all. It's nice.

Sometimes those contented moments hit away from home. They crystallize in my mind with the exact clarity of the moment and cannot be altered. At a graveside on a hill in southern Ohio, the day was gray. Jillian, Jacob, and I worked near the gravestone, tucking in geraniums and verbena, pulling out the start of poison ivy. English ivy that I planted years ago had covered the base of the stone, making it both more anchored and firm. By 11:00 the clouds had thickened. At noon we heard — a minute before we felt — the pelting rainfall. It swept like a tidal wave across the hill to the west, across the valley soaking the Holsteins and the grass, then up past the yucca plants along the cemetery fence, and onto us. We got very wet. But the rain passed as quickly as it came, and we dried in a short time.

The three of us ate our lunch down the hill near graves of unknown Swiss ancestors. My brother's family — Nett, Jess, Kate, Jim — joined us that afternoon. For a long time the seven of us sat on the hill and said nothing and did nothing. A bell like the Angelus chimed 5 o'clock from the church far below the cemetery, the church where my great-grandfather used to preach. Then my two nieces and Jacob put orange trumpet vine flowers on their fingers and pretended they were witches, and we went home.

Contentment strikes like that in unexpected places, when you are vaguely aware, without really knowing, that there is no place else you would rather be. Nothing mattered that day but the two families gathered, long dead ancestors, and the view of hillsides covered with corn and cows. Nothing matters today but Huckle who is now asleep in the flower bed and the geese who have slipped over the creek embankment. Their heads disappear from my sight to scoop up water, then rise above the ferns. The geese turn their wet bills skyward to swallow.

And the earth turns and the sun shines, occasionally illuminating that inexplicable connection between a moment in a day and the knowledge that there is no place else I would rather be.

Blue
August, 1993

I had lived almost 35 years before I saw a bluebird. The wait was worth it. With uncommon beauty the bird that first landed in my back yard beside the roiling-gray ocean was unconcerned about his striking appearance. He took his blue for granted. I, on the other hand, was stunned by his color, believing a piece of the sky had broken off and tumbled down into my yard. Like Chicken Little, I wanted to tell the king, or at least my family, that the sky had truly fallen.

Never, since that bird's arrival when the heavens came to my feet, have I looked at blue in nature the same way. The appearance of that color in birds, flowers, and insects is like discovering a rare sapphire, a jewel of exquisite and delicate beauty.

Finding "blue" brings a moment of peace and delight when I am engulfed with the need to use my eyes and soak up the color. I love blue sky overhead — where it belongs, smiling with a grin that announces "today is the perfect afternoon for floating in a pond on the raft, captured under a tent of blue." That's summer.

But blue on the wing is bewitching. Someone puts a magic spell on me, and I remember forever the "first blues." In South Dakota at the edge of a prairie, there, suddenly, clinging to a goldenrod stalk, was a fat, deep blue, large-beaked bird, looking very much like one of my common winter visitors, the evening grosbeak, dipped in a bucket of blue paint. He was so big and bold, swaying in the prairie wind, that I was rendered speechless at his arrival, and then let loose a flurry of thoughtless shouts, "Look, Look, Look there!" all of which served to frighten the blue grosbeak away. But I had seen him.

Another time, in southern Manitoba, Jake saw a mountain bluebird. I missed him — and any others that might have been around, in spite of checking the miles of boxes nailed to barbed wire fence posts at the edge of wheat fields. I was envious of Jake's sighting and pouted all week. I never saw one.

Had it not been for the isolation and peace of the back roads in Amish country in Ohio, I would have missed my first indigo bunting who flew quickly across the road in front of my car. But I had time to stop, get out, and look above me on the telephone wires, hearing only the rustle of wind in the tall corn fields chanting "blue, blue indigo" while the bunting looked back at me.

"First blues" give way to continuing blues, and my mind catalogs the charm of subsequent bluebirds — regular nestings in our yard, the male hunting each evening from a dead limb in the ash tree out front. We won't cut off the unsightly branch, for it serves as the bluebirds' favored perching spot. I remember 50 bluebirds perched along power wires above a huge expanse of a grassy dam in Tennessee. And to think it had taken me 35 years to see only one.

Lately, there have been no blue jays at our feeder, and, although the bluebird family of at least four juveniles in the front yard has atoned for the jays' absence, I miss their daily raucous arrival, the bullies of the blue-color-world, who rather enjoy calling attention to themselves.

In my garden this year, I have tried a new blue flower, *Nigella*, "love-in-a-mist," that Ruth, a fellow gardener, showed me last year. It is a feathery-like plant, so fringed and intertwined that it too could be the result of witchcraft, a tricky plant in which it is hard to determine where the stalk ends and leaves begin. The blossoms themselves are round button-like affairs. *Nigella's* total disregard for normal flower ways emphasizes to me that blue flowers are different — and surely quite rare.

Growing among the pinks, reds, oranges, and yellows of calendula and zinnias, cleome and nicotiana in my garden are brilliant blue cornflowers. Their Latin name, *Centaurea cyanus*, reflects two legends which tell of the importance and the naming of this flower. Cyanus was a young Greek who loved Chloris, the goddess of flowers. He collected cornflowers for her alter daily because of the beauty of the blue color. When, one day, Chloris found Cyanus dead in a field of these blue flowers, she was so moved by his devotion that she changed his body into a cornflower and gave it his name.

The Greeks, who knew much about medicinal properties of plants, also tell the story of the centaur Chiron who was wounded by an arrow that was covered with poisonous blood from Hydra. Chiron bandaged the arrow injury with masses of cornflowers which rapidly healed the wound; thus the genus *Centaurea*.

By our pond chicory grows. At last, I sigh. I have missed my huge garden of chicory that grew at our ocean-side farm. There, in the month of August, a wild riot of blue covered the edge of the road. In the night yellow and black argiope spiders spun webs that at dawn caught sunlight on the dew dripping from silver strands. The blue flowers opened their eyes and gazed at the sun. At noon when the spider webs were dry, the goldfinches chattered their way in and around the flower stems, reflecting the sunshine in their colors, yellow dancing with blue.

I used to spend hours watching the goings-on in my chicory garden and now, perhaps again I will be lucky enough to have this blue-color-dance nearby, an old friend moving with me to a new place. My pond chicory is small, only a few plants, but there are more than last year and I am hopeful.

I once read a fable about chicory, like the Greek myths of cornflowers. The petals of the blossom look like rays of the sun in the color blue. This Rumanian tale told of Florilor, lady of flowers, who was gentle and beautiful. The sun god, who was attracted to her but did not intend to marry her, came to earth to woo Florilor who turned him away. In his anger he lashed out and turned her into the flower chicory, one who watches the sun all day and mirrors the form of the sun with her many rays, the petals. I don't know if I like this tale or not. And yet it does convey the feeling I have had for a long time about the magic of blue.

My pond is home, too, for damselflies and dragonflies with iridescent blue bodies. They are never still for a moment and even when I am as motionless as the jeweled frogs that bask in the sunshine on the pond's muddy banks, I cannot do more than catch a glimpse of brilliant blue, darting swiftly among the cattails. Like other blues, this one is a bewitching color which brings on magic charms and bouts of downright ecstasy in the observer, me.

Today is the time to be watching for those blues of August, the ones that delight and surprise me, bedazzle and mesmerize me, and always leave me smiling when I get the "blues."

Garden visitors
September, 1993

Our garden is just about perfect now. It's a shame, too, because the inevitable frost lurks just around the corner, the bogeyman waiting to snatch our hard-earned gold. Maybe if he had a use for cosmos and tomatoes, I wouldn't mind so much, but his hand brings only black and decay.

While I wait for frost to strike, I spend my free minutes each day wandering up and down the garden rows, like a shopper in a huge department store, clipping marigolds or broccoli shoots, eating the autumn raspberries, digging carrots.

Today, I am harvesting the dried flowers — globe amaranth and statice. Harvest time is like watching your children go off to lives of their own. The little seeds, unknown, or seedlings raised during March's blizzards on a snug windowsill, were set with care into the soil in June — to flourish on their own. Of course I helped. I weeded and watered, fertilized and fussed a bit here and there, but in general the plants grew to be things I could not direct.

My white statice, for instance, is abundant. But in March I also planted statice of "mixed bold colors," bright lavender, rose and blue colors, which I hoped would add flair to my dried bouquets. But they didn't do well. I have mostly white. Last year, pink amaranth grew; this year only white and deep purple thrive, one of the surprises of gardening — or child rearing. "The best laid plans of mice and men," I think to myself.

I like the garden in autumn better than any other time of year because of its abundance and preciousness. So little time is left to relish these fruits. "If I can hold on to these cucumbers and calendulas just a few more weeks," I whisper to the frost gods.

Life is abundant now in the garden. Everywhere among the sunflowers are goldfinches with their persistent call, up and down like their flight pattern, sprinkling these September days with a dash of pepper-black wings, spicing the moment.

On the zinnias, grasshoppers of every sort pause. Unlike grasshoppers of summer, these do not flee, but hold a pose so I can watch them. The first looks like a mosaic, one piece of tile-like exoskeleton placed against another, a chain mail protection. Zinnia-leafed green with black stripes on the head, this one watches me with one of his multiple eyes. Below him on the stem near the base of the plant is a much larger version of the first grasshopper. I wonder what makes the size difference. Age? A slightly different species?

My field guide suggests they may be red-legged locust — pests. Or maybe they are alutacea bird grasshoppers (Latin name of *Schistocerca alutacea*, makes me smile). I can only remember the red legs when I am inside researching. Over 1000 species of orthoptera exist in North America alone, so who in the world really knows who is visiting my zinnias today?

There is another species of grasshopper on the cornflowers, a tiny delicate creature, the kind a maiden aunt would approve of for its obvious polite manners. This little grasshopper daintily chews and moves on after wiping her mouth.

My field guide lists other grasshoppers with spiritual names like green valley grasshopper, a name that makes me think of peaceful coexistence of insect and plant life; still another is called horse lubber grasshopper, which sounds like a creature who surely would be found on Western ranges. There are crazy names, too, like Nebraska cone-head, a type of katydid whose range includes Maine, and creosote bush grasshopper, who doesn't live here.

The field crickets, of course, are everywhere — even in the house. Every time I catch one indoors, I am tempted to let him stay — the old Chinese belief of good luck and all that. Outdoors, they are like children at a county fair, sampling a bit of everything. Now as autumn comes on they will seek humidity and shelter from frost under the canopy of bean plants, beet greens, and towering stalks of dill. I like crickets, especially their incessant trill of autumn, which, like spring toads' song, indicates everything is working on schedule.

While I'm inspecting grasshoppers and crickets, a short squat bumblebee stumbles through, tripping over the stamen on the butterscotch-colored zinnia. At my feet a woolly bear caterpillar rolls quickly into a ball at my intrusion, and then unrolls and scrambles off, searching for dark caverns under tomato branches. Over my head, two white cabbage butterflies play tag.

As if orchestrated, a flock of song sparrows rises from the corn stalks, moving just a short distance into the raspberry thicket as I approach. They'll wait there until I harvest corn for dinner and then return to pick at weed seeds. Our garden has plenty of those.

This evening the three of us eat our harvest — one vegetable after another. I know my son longs for hamburgers, but this isn't a meat day. Two turkey vultures swoop low, surprising us, looking for meat, too, as they circle over our porch, the closest I've ever seen them come here. I remember years ago when I saw these birds only in Ohio. But all things change, even the expanding territory of birds, and autumn is coming on once again, bringing with it the seasonal changes.

It is dusk now, and I am reminded that the autumn light is changing, angling toward a slow-down, a completion. Time to move indoors. But not yet, not this month. Hang on just a little longer, walk the garden paths a few more weeks. Eat one more handful of raspberries. Pull a few weeds. Husk corn. See who else has come to call.

Dogs go to town
February, 1994

I like the village where I live. I especially like it on Saturday mornings, and I am convinced that the dogs of this town like that part of the week, too. Every Saturday, beginning somewhere around 8:30 in the morning and ending about noon, when the post office and library close, all around the country roads and the village streets, the dogs of Bowdoinham hear the call, "Come on Spot, wanna go to the store?"

If the call hasn't been sounded, the dog has tuned in to the activity. The car is being loaded with trash, well, not exactly trash, this is recyclable stuff, but to dogs in general, and our dog in particular, it makes no difference.

In the morning hours on Saturday, all dogs in town — all pedigrees, shapes, colors, personalities, those of little brains and even a few smart ones, registered or unregistered — enjoy the same outing. There are five places to go. If the dog is real lucky, he will get to visit three spots. If the day bodes exceedingly fine, all five beehives of activity will be hit.

For Casey, our golden retriever, who is such a doofus, Saturday morning is the culmination of the dream. Last Saturday was no different. I loaded the cab and back of the truck with all the cardboard, wastepaper, mixed tin cans and numbers 1 and 2 plastic, all newspapers, and Christmas catalogs that I could find still lying around the house. She watched me with perceptive eyes. It was a stretch for her brain, but yeah, she got the idea. Aha. Recycling time. This must be Saturday morning. Ta Da!!

Laden with library books, thank you notes and graduate school applications as yet unmailed, pizza trays we had borrowed the night before from the Town Landing store (complete with uncooked pizza), and a note to myself to remember to buy the Saturday newspaper, I walked out the door. Casey was on my heels and beat me to the car door, covering the thirteen feet in a split second. I couldn't go without her.

I knew it and had saved a little corner of the seat, in-between the low grade recyclable paper bags and the bin of newspapers. I gave her a boost, and we were off.

The recycling barn was a bundle of activity — my friend Judith's new dog, a brindle lurcher, sat politely, shivering in the damp cold wind, minding her manners as we chatted. In spite of her breed's reputation as a poacher, she knew how to behave on her Saturday morning jaunt. She was the perfect visitor to town. I expected her to be wearing white gloves.

At the post office, our next stop, the black lab sitting behind the steering wheel of the equally black pickup fooled me for a moment. With his shoulders hunched forward and his unmoving stare, directed straight ahead into the post office window — if he had been wearing a White Sox cap — he could have passed for the driver. His Saturday mornings were obviously intense, worrisome. "Is my master coming back? I won't let him out of my sight." But his demeanor was offset by the eager behavior coming from behind the truck's bucket seats. There a chocolate lab, her head swiveling right to left, kept the action lively. "Hey look, there's that doofus of a golden retriever. Told you she comes here every week. Look, there's a mutt trundling over the hill, following right at his master's heels. What a groveler! Haven't seen him before. Must be new in town."

At the restaurant where we were returning pizza racks, a black mutt with short ears stared down toward the river, perhaps dreaming of summer romps on the grass and in the water. She had a hot pink bandana tied around her neck, all decked out in her Saturday-go-to-town outfit.

At the store where we picked up the paper and milk, the parking lot was alive with dogs — multi-colored mutts in 4 x 4s, slobbering on windows as they greeted each other, a respectable spaniel who waited patiently, curled up on the back seat of a respectable car, and an unkempt shaggy collie-cross who yipped at everyone. Casey had a ball running from one side of the truck to the other. "Yea, this is what life is all about — Saturday morning and a lot of dogs to think about for the whole week."

Our last stop was the library where we found a dour-looking Doberman who seemed to think outings meant one more thing to protect. But Casey just smiled at him. "Hey, fellow, don't take life too seriously. Nothing like a ride into the village to get the blood going. Beats a walk in the fresh air any day."

A touch of grace
May, 1994

Back in the woods, north of the house and hidden from view by tangles of blackberry, bittersweet vine, and red maple saplings which clutch at each other like forbidden lovers, is an old ice pond, fed by waters which rise to earth in spots, forming a swale. Once, farmers of this land created this pond and cut their winter's supply of ice from it.

Its working purpose long gone now, the ice pond has become a sanctuary, a hallowed open spot where the heavens rise above the outstretched arms of maples, and the sky is reflected in the inky blackness of the pond below. It is here that the psalm is sung when the the month of May arrives. It is here that I go, seeking grace, seeking peace.

On one edge of the pond, just below the earth berm, an embankment created by hands long since laid to rest, the remains of a road, wide enough for a horse-drawn vehicle, travel into the darkness of the woods beyond. Immediately south of and parallel to this road is a stone wall where the vines and trees intertwine. It is at this crossroads of sorts, places where people once worked and passed by and where the swale runs heavy enough with water in all seasons except summer's end, that I find the beginnings of May and the touch of grace that is the hallmark of this season.

Nestled into the base of the stone wall are clusters of red trillium, foul-smelling flowers I have been told, but I have yet to notice. I think of these delicate beauties as wake-robins, the other name by which they are called. They may not smell with the sweetness of spring, nor are they red either, but a deep royal ruby, yet these delicate dancing blossoms appear as the first fragile overtures to May.

Background music to this psalm is the chorus of spring peepers and wood frogs and the trilling notes of the toads. These now-threatened creatures abound in this leaf-filled water world of the old pond, taking their refuge and giving life in the underwater nurseries. I cannot imagine spring without their music anymore than I can imagine it without the songs of the birds.

Overhead are warblers of infinite delight and color and melody — cerulean blue parula warblers, rich chestnut-sided warblers, shocking, neon yellowthroat warblers. A scarlet tanager passes by this pond. A pair of mallards stops for respite. The ovenbird scratches nearby. The flute of a wood thrush echoes behind me. The symphony is at a crescendo; the psalm is written with a flourish.

"For lo, the winter is past, the rain is over and gone. The flowers appear on the earth, and the time of the singing of birds is come."

Truly, it is now that the land is alive — and it is only for these few short weeks that the land will remain so. Each morning leaves grow bigger. Tadpoles develop swiftly hurrying before their ice pond is too shallow; the blazing orange oriole courts his mate, wooing her with color and song. Once they have nested, they will be subdued and almost invisible to my eyes.

Insects are hatching, swarming, multiplying. I itch and scratch at the thought, but it is this activity, too, that allows the swoop of the great-creasted flycatcher as he returns to his perch and calls from the swaying birch at the pond's edge.

One May, in this spot, Jake and I sat on the pond's dam, the western sun rays to our back, lost in our thoughts, when a rustle at the other side of the pond caught our attention. Lumbering, dragging its magnificent tail behind it, a beaver appeared as if by magic from the swale's tangled vegetation and slipped into the pond. He swam straight toward us, his head sleek and blackened by the water. We did not move. He turned, swam back, turned again, repeating his routine. We waited a long time, before slipping quietly onto the woods road and leaving the beaver to his solitude in our sanctuary.

How many Mays do we each have in a life time, I often wonder? How many beavers or scarlet tanagers will we see? Will there ever be enough? Can I compose enough psalms to the beauty of this month? There is no other month in which I, the winter weary traveler, find such solace in the collective air around me. Surely it must be that way for all travelers. Somewhere, tucked either in memory or still accessible, is a sanctuary for each of us where hymns are sung to May.

On skunks and chickens
November, 1994

Because of the early darkness, a minor crisis occurs here each evening. About 6:30 one of us suddenly realizes that we have not yet closed up the chicken coop. This coop houses the privileged chickens on our farm, the tiny Cochin and Silkie fowl who spend their days in a wildly exciting variety of activities. At dusk, however, all merriment comes to an end, and they retire, 33 in number, to the "poultry palace" for the night. Sometime after that point, it is our job to run outside — and slam and lock a door.

The big barn chickens do not get this protection. They come and go in a sheltered area, but must beware of fox or raccoon, for they are on their own. Coop chicks, however, get loving care.

During the day, all 33 roam the front yard, the side yard, the wooded area near their coop. This summer, on one of those courageous journeys into the woods, the entire flock was surprised by a coyote, leaping through the underbrush. I have never seen such a wild, hysterical squawking, followed by Kamikaze chickens swooping in low. It took us all afternoon to locate the six newly-hatched chicks who had frozen, either out of fear or instinct, and refused to move as if they had been turned to stone.

They sometimes travel en masse to the pond, but they never venture farther east than that. They slip through the fence that surrounds the garden and peck at tomatoes and cabbage worms. Under the bird feeders, they gorge themselves on dropped sunflower seeds. They perch on the stone walls that fence their coop from the basketball court, looking like a gathering of old men on park benches. In midwinter they migrate to the front porch and huddle on this south-facing exposure, cackling and crowing to each other all day. Idle feathers make idle brains, I believe. They don't care.

Their personalities are as different as their activities. There are actually 34 chickens, but one, Dusty, a rooster, roosts in the garage, either an elitist or an outcast. Furball acts like a football coach, issuing instructions and commands to his harem. When he isn't doing that, he chases Zoot, who prides himself on his suit of iridescent green. Velveteen teaches other hens how to mother. Chicken Little, the matriarch of the flock, rules from her perch, content to wile away the hours looking out the window. Addie refuses to lay her eggs in normal places, like under geraniums. She prefers the fourth step on the way to the attic. Little Leaf is the single, newly hatched chick who looks very much out of place dressed in yellow down in November. Chicks are April events, but these chickens will nest anytime, and faithful and true, they wait for results.

Perhaps it is a combination of these characteristics — steadfastness and liveliness — that moves us to have such a concern for these chickens. Be that as it may, we never go to bed without closing the coop, late as we may be in remembering to do so.

Therefore, it was with no small amount of apprehension that this fall we realized that someone, actually two someones, were moving into the coop at dusk. A pile of scat next to the feed bin sparked a niggling concern. I had a reason to worry. One October evening I stepped into the coop and was greeted by two skunks, both curled into balls, nose to tail like woolly bear caterpillars, napping before supper right beside two egg-laying hens. I politely backed out the door. It took us an hour of banging on the coop walls to roust those two.

After that experience, we carefully examined the coop from the outside first, turning on the light, peering through the dusty windows, craning our necks to inspect all corners where a black and white skunk might dine on a supper of scrambled eggs.

There are plenty of those lying around the coop floor, maybe 26 this very day. The hens sit on piles in various manners, at some point finally deciding to establish an official nest. Before that point, however, any self-respecting skunk would have no problem finding a feast night after night. This feasting went on unabated in spite of my ritual. I would call loudly as I approached the coop, bang on the windows, and wait a few moments for any unwelcome guest to vacate the premises, a bit like letting the boyfriend escape by the back door. On occasion I saw the larger one scurrying to hide under the coop. It was never a fast escape, as the burrow entrance was made by rabbits for rabbits, and he always got stuck part way in, at which point he had to wiggle and tug a bit. That was always an unsettling part of this routine because the wiggling and tugging part was inevitably performed with his rear end and tail sticking out in my direction.

After weeks of this — and a long conversation with my veterinarian sister who warned me about rabid skunks — I decided it might be well to discourage the varmints. We had captured skunks before in the Hav-A-Hart trap, but definitely by accident with near catastrophic results. I would not purposefully plan to trap a skunk. The alternative was to close the coop immediately when the last chicken scurried in the door at dusk.

To do this I had to pay attention and be prompt. I also had to be home from work at dusk, a feat not always possible. As darkness came on earlier and earlier, I struggled to do this, with some success. But, in fact, I was also becoming complacent. I hadn't seen the skunk for a week, so on one night in early November I innocently tackled this chore, not bothering with precautions. I was also, for some foolish reason, wearing shorts and sandals.

I stepped into the little alcove leading to the door, the place where the bins of food are stored. My footsteps must have echoed like giants for there was a sudden flurry of little toenails scraping plywood and a general explosion of panic, not unlike an exploding bottle of ink. He — yes, he was eating egg on the half shell — flew across my feet and between my legs. Skunk fur on my bare legs! Skunk toes on my toes! In retrospect I was struck by how coarse his fur felt, but at that moment I thought I might die. This close encounter with a skunk was too much. His heart may have been beating fast, caught in the act of thievery, but my heart was beating faster.

I continued to shriek long after he had disappeared around the back of the coop. Either he was getting too fat to go down the tunnel quickly, or the elevated cholesterol levels had addled his brain and he no longer knew the escape route. Whatever, he hasn't been back and I, all the wiser, now send Jake to do the coop closing chore.

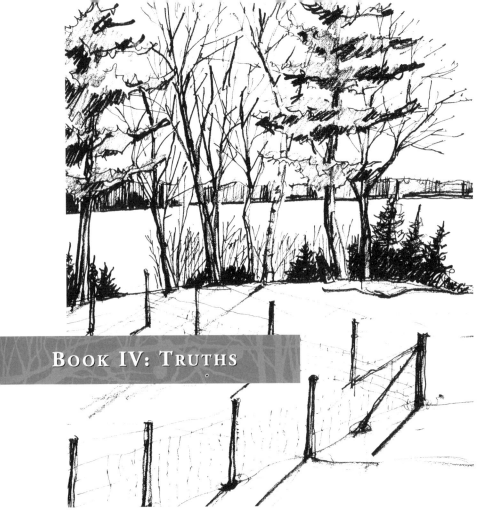

BOOK IV: TRUTHS

Celebrate winter with a walk
December, 1994

Brittle, gleaming days. Frigid, deep space cold nights. Winter's beauty is stark and clear, a metal etching created by gifted artists of the Far North on display for a few months. I tend to observe the artwork from behind closed doors and curtained windows, with only an occasional peek between the blinds to reassure myself that nothing has changed, that I am still in awe of the intricacies of the snowflake, the rainbows of icicles. But to actually spend much time walking among this artistry — well, no thanks, I like my fireside better, and besides I'm too old to sled.

And so I snuggle down in my new recliner where my conscience and my memory gnaw at my muscles, urging me to get up and outside. "You need the exercise. Don't you recall," my mind inquires, "wonderful walks in winter? And aren't there more to be had. Time is a-wasting." I squirm, but memory alone isn't enough. What about intrigue?

There are four full moons in winter — December is the Cold Moon, January, the Wolf Moon, February, the Hunger Moon, and March, only days before the spring equinox, is the Sap Moon. The names of these moons, tied to folklore and Indian knowledge, are compelling. Surely I want to be outside on those nights, to explore the riddles of the winter moons, to walk in their glow.

And I remember the wonders of winter walks at night.

Not so many years ago, when the snow was brilliant white and the sky jet black, when the Hunger Moon washed all shadows with silver, I took a small child to explore. He had insisted we go out, that it had never been so bright outside. He assured me I would be glad. He was right.

Booted and mittened, we trampled the perimeter of our land, wandering into the sheep pasture which lay under unbroken snow, creating a puff pillow for giant heads. Our breath turned to water droplets, which froze on the scarves wrapped tightly around our faces. Our shadows followed us wherever we walked, attached to our heels as if afraid to desert us. I whispered to my small son that I would not like to be a mouse on such a night. This time, I was right, for soon we crossed the traces of a drama in the hollow where the cinnamon ferns grow in summer. There, the outline of owl wing tips was pressed upon the face of the snow, tail feathers fanned behind wings. Tiny footprints left the point of impact and vanished into air. We shuddered as we imagined the attack. We looked cautiously over our own shoulders, wary and excited.

And don't I recall a January meadow?

This time on skis with the smallest of girls, I took her across acres of hay fields, our destination the neighbor's lambing barn. It was a sugar-crystal January night, with only inky blackness behind, but her eyes, closer to the ground than mine, found wonders in the meadow. "Queen Anne's lace are all stars," she said. She urged me to look at dried stalks, stems as fragile as strings of ribbon candy, topped with lace flowers, dry shapes against the snow. She found the spot where wild strawberries grow and her imagination brought back summer days. And under the glow of the Wolf Moon we thought for a moment we heard coyotes cry.

And there were nights of fire, too.

That night the Cold Moon looked like a newly-minted silver dollar, flooding the fields with riches. A bonfire flickered in the distant woods south of the stone wall, the result of the day's clearing efforts, and a ward against the temperature. We needed no flashlight, for the trees stood like stone offerings to the gods, thin and unyielding, allowing moonlight to penetrate the forest. Our shadows danced like spirits, wickedly leaping at us, snatching our hats from our heads by pretending to be low-hanging branches.

Three of us held hands that night. Two others brought the discarded remains of our Christmas tree and threw them into the bonfire. Dying ashes whirled above our heads and danced back to earth. The fire calmed. We walked home following the stream, plucking at prickle bushes and broken goldenrod stems that clog the stream in summer. The beehive was visible. The paper wasp nest in the maple hung like a dew drop. The trail of a weasel was stitched along the stone wall. Everything was precise and clear in the moonlight.

And now that I am indoors...

I wonder what happens to those nights of exploration and adventure when we get older. Why don't we still take midnight skis, dance in the snow, build bonfires? Why do we no longer play? Perhaps a combination of memory and intrigue, sprinkled liberally with the fear of growing set in my ways, will lure me out the door this December.

If I don't follow the moons, surely this winter I can walk the road with the dog, or build a snowman in the front yard. Days of sunshine, bright as beach days, will entice me outside, to walk and breathe deeply the richness of air no longer mingled with pollen and summer dust. My lungs will be scrubbed clean, my body invigorated and tingling with the cold. I will take time to mark the trails of field mice and the cold, crisp call of chickadees. I will delight in the sparkle and wonder of snowflakes by daylight or, perhaps, under the richness of winter's full moons.

Spring signs
March, 1995

Is there any month as long and as erratic as March? Is there any interval as endless as "mud" season? When our children were little, we survived the thirty-one long days of March with a contest — hunting for signs of spring. The object was simple: find a spring sign and be the first one home to write it on the calendar. Add a sticker, usually flowers or rabbits or something equally appealing to a five year old, and soon the month of March was filled — and April had arrived.

I still have some of those old calendar months of March lying around. March first always had something written into the little square: "a fly in the kitchen," or "bird song." By midweek entries like "first bike ride," or "running water," or "first duck egg laid" would appear. And by mid-March it got better: "red-winged blackbird at feeder" and "skunk smell!" and "ice cream cone" or simply "sunshine." Just before the official arrival of spring someone would write "first robin" and after March 22 I find "maple syrup trip" and "ice out." Children's scrawls filled these old calendars; their laborious letters read "killdeer, pussy willows, wild geese off shore at Clark Island," and "purple and yellow crocuses in front yard."

Yet no event seems to mark the season of spring as much as the notation "lamb born." The first year we ever kept sheep, some 19 years ago, we were naive in our husbandry. We had purchased two lambs that summer. One went to slaughter in the fall; Cassie we kept and in our ignorance never suspected that she might be pregnant. Winter went on. We fed her and loved her. Of all the sheep we ever owned, she still remains my favorite.

Then, on March 17, 1976, when I opened the small barn door to do the evening chores, there stood a delightful Suffolk-looking lamb (the spitting image of the ram Chester who had gone to market), alert and pert, beside her mother. For a moment I was transported beyond reality into a world of bewilderment. Was I seeing correctly? Where once there was one, now there were two. Even now, years later, I can still resurrect the total astonishment I felt. A true sense of awe descended on the barn and the meaning of spring and rebirth stood in front of me. When the lamb baaed, I recovered and raced back to the house shouting, "Cassie has a baby!"

We named her Shamrock and she grew up to give us many offspring, one of whom gave birth to a white ewe this very morning. Perhaps she should be named for her great (many times over) grandmother.

The arrival of lambs has become routine around our farm now. We are no longer surprised when ewes have single or twin births. We expect we will feed one or two in the house, and the baby bottles are ready. We know we have tails to dock and nursing ewes to attend to. It's part of the shepherding.

Lambing begins sometimes as early as January and keeps on until March, depending on the year. But repetition does not take away the miracle and the feeling of renewal, and in spite of mud and gloom, unpredicted snows and sleet, lambs promise that the world is opening up again, their hops and skips signifying that carefree days are here.

But this March we learned that complacency leaves us easy prey. We were ambushed by white ewe number 89 when she delivered black ram triplets. Cute, inquisitive and spindly, these three bundles of tightly coiled lamb fleece slipped into the beginning of spring. Only once since 1976 have we had triplets, and then one died almost immediately. In the genealogy of miracles, those triplets were born to the daughter of Shamrock. These triplets are a new family line and all three will make it.

We anticipated we would have to supplement their feeding, but surprisingly enough, no one required "house care." The smallest and softest of the three looks more like a licorice jelly bean with legs than a lamb. He is tiny, yet drinks reluctantly from the bottle. His middle-sized brother, however, is greedy for his turn, quite taken with extra milk, and he chews eagerly on our boot laces, while we feed his tinier brother.

The largest of the three ignores us, for he is busy playing king of the hay bales, a game with rules that only lambs understand. Sixteen others challenge his position, wanting themselves to be king or queen for the morning, as he scrambles to the top of the hay mountain. There he balances on four fragile legs and dares the others to push him off.

To frolic like this in the sunshine is not only the prerogative of lambs. It is their duty as well. They are the heralds of spring and, with that designation, deserve the most important spot on the March calendar.

Birding with a friend
May, 1995

For almost 20 months of May now, my friend Heather and I have ventured forth at the crack of dawn in search of birds. The ritual has become so ingrained that, although we may not see each other for weeks, when the phone rings and she answers there is no need for small talk. "Wanna go tomorrow?" she asks after I say hi.

"I'll be there by six," I reply. We hang up.

She lives in town and we begin there, scouring her weeping hemlock and inspecting her blueberry bushes to see if they have survived the winter and her son's mowing habits. We discuss her groundhog problems, her diminished root crop last year, all the while scanning the branches above with our binoculars. We do not need to look at each other to communicate. In the middle of sentences, words like "yellow-rumped on that outer limb" slip from our mouths. We are two of a kind. We could watch one yellow-rumped warbler all morning. Each spring we are startled by the richness of color, the newness of a species. Together and alone in the wee hours of Saturday morning we watch and count our birds.

The weather — cold, raw almost to the point that we wish for our mittens — foggy, too, is perhaps the worst kind for birding. Rain is imminent.

We leave her backyard and walk to the Androscoggin River. There the fog is worse. We need cormorants to add to our list. In spite of the beauty and joy of the hunt, we are also keenly competitive counters — competitive, that is, only with ourselves. From year to year we compile our lists, saving and comparing, and always shooting for a goal.

The river reveals nothing but pigeons on the bridge beams and one lone great blue heron, shrouded like a ghost rising from the waters, standing on one leg on a ledge.

We hurry back to the car, driving out of town and along the edge of another river. We pause at a farm overlooking Merrymeeting Bay. The farmer comes out of his barn, early morning chores complete. We wave, admire his donkey, scan the field for killdeer. We stop at a cove along the Bay.

"This is the perfect habitat. It should be alive."

I agree with her, but we find very little — the weather hampering us. In the distance, a ruffed grouse drums, our ears picking up what our eyes cannot see.

On to the Muddy River — along the way we snag a mockingbird — and for us the treat of the day, barn swallows refusing to fly. They sit and let us admire the shades of rust and red and brick on their breasts, like badges of courage. Two little ones lift their wings, picking at feathers one by one, grooming and displaying. We climb into the car, drive on to my farm.

"Birding has made me so much more aware," Heather says.

It is true. We notice much in our few hours together, hungry for more — last year a beaver by the small pond we regularly visit — this year the awakening buds of red trillium. We witness a yellow-bellied sapsucker, intent on attracting a mate if not us. His antics, hammering at full speed on a metal lamp post and moving to the metal tags on the side of a telephone pole, confuse us. We hear him shriek in spite of the guide book's declaration that this voice should be "quiet." I am certain I have run over one of the chickens on our farm, but it is only the sapsucker's cry. He is not following the rules. We laugh, noting his success with the arrival of a prospective mate on the apple tree.

The warblers are few and far between this day. Last year we saw pine, black-throated green, parula, and chestnut-sided ones. This year we see only the yellow-rumped and hear the ovenbird and black-and-white. Last year we watched — and easily identified — a blue-headed vireo. This year there are no such coups. We have to hearken back to the first blue-gray gnatcatcher either of us saw at a woods-meadow margin in 1980. We're like that together. Remembering big achievements.

We worry a little bit, too. "I haven't seen a towhee for years," she tells me and my concern rises. It's true for me, and I live where birds abound. It's unsettling.

Our bird lists have changed, too. We no longer go to the head of Maquoit Bay but in those days our lists included willets and green herons in 1976, semi-palmated plovers and snowy egrets in 1977. Now we look for kinglets, least flycatchers, and bluebirds.

We see nor hear none on this fog-encased day, 1995. But it doesn't matter. We have the brilliant yellow of a meadowlark, the antics of that sapsucker, the gentle paddling of a mallard to carry us through until the first Saturday in May, next year — same time, same place.

A groundhog truce
June, 1995

The only time I ever saw my grandfather with a shotgun was the time he shot the groundhog. There's a popular picture in our family archives of him holding the shotgun — the butt resting on the ground — in one hand and the short, bushy tail of that woodchuck in his other hand. He has a grin on his face. My grandpa wasn't known for having a grin on his face.

My mother recalls that as far as grandpa was concerned, that groundhog in the garden was "not good." Grandpa prided himself on what he grew. His grandparents had arrived from Switzerland a generation earlier with the love of the land and cultivating crops burning in their blood. Grandpa's flowers and vegetables carried forth that tradition, but creatures like groundhogs, who in one evening destroyed his entire broccoli patch, just could not be tolerated.

I was brought back to that shotgun picture the other day, when my son Jake and I happened upon two little groundhogs playing in the middle of the road. We swerved to avoid hitting them, and after we passed and stopped to look back, they went about their afternoon June romp as if no large red monster had suddenly appeared over the horizon, almost ending their short lives. They scurried one way, then back the other. Their noses touched; they huddled close together and whispered woodchuck secrets, maybe wondering why they are called such diverse names as "groundhog" and "woodchuck," though I'm sure grandpa could explain the hog part.

I know where stuffed animal manufacturers get their inspiration. One look at those groundhogs and I know all young mammals can be transformed into something cute and cuddly. Those two chocolate brown scamps were a far cry from the thirty pound garden-destroyer that swung by the tail from grandpa's hand.

Groundhogs have always been the epitome of the first real sign of spring to me. Beginning in late March I comb the highway median strips looking for famished woodchucks emerging and chomping down on whatever blades of fresh new grass they can find. I never see them in March. Some years I never see them until late April, but once I do, I spend the rest of the spring driving with one eye on the grass, looking to spot a groundhog. I'm not sure what the appeal is. I can't really see eyes or mouth and, therefore, have no idea what sort of disposition the groundhog has. But still, I like to find signs of nature's routine continuing unabated in spite of my time schedule, which includes traveling at 65 mph.

Once I might have thought them to be mean mammals. When my children cornered a full grown groundhog in a front yard and the creature snapped and growled, I was ignorant enough to think groundhogs were ferocious. Now I know that is not true. Defense against children armed with hockey sticks demands growling.

The frustrating part of dealing with groundhogs is that these fellows aren't content with green grass and clover sprigs. What drives them into gardens for cultivated carrot tops? Why must they eat all the new spinach leaves? That's where the rub comes in, why my friend is frantically trapping "her" groundhog, and why, forty years ago, grandpa shot his. Overnight, months of effort, not to mention a family's food supply, is gone, while the groundhog has at his disposal, acres of green growing things that we humans do not compete for.

A few years ago I had my first one-on-one encounter with a young groundhog. He, too, sat in the middle of the road — I wonder what's with adolescent woodchucks' fascination with roads — but this time the road was gravel and seldom traveled. I stopped the car, rolled down the window, and spoke to him. He just stared at me, his black beady eyes inquisitive and curious. I can almost remember that he cocked his head as if to ask me to repeat what I said. It was an odd sort of experience, talking to a wild creature who stayed and listened.

I told him how charming he was, and then politely asked that he not travel too far up the road and discover that I, too, had a garden. I warned him about grandpa's groundhog's demise. I felt like Mrs. Cottontail warning Peter not to go to Farmer MacGregor's garden. I neglected to tell him that I didn't have a shotgun.

Loss
October, 1995

Living on a farm is sometimes more about loss than it is about birth and growing things. I have never been a lover of autumn. October, for all its brilliance and truly peaceful days of cricket song and aster dances, leaves me a little cautious. I know it is the end. I don't want to be deceived by the glory.

This autumn played no such tricks, no deception. Perhaps it was the effect of the drought that drove predators out of the deep woods, looking for food and water, but whatever the cause, the predation was without pretense. As we lost one animal after another, there was no course of action except to watch.

Death is part of the process, and eight years ago when we released Bun from her cage, we knew the chances. But a life lived freely, albeit more dangerously, seemed preferable to a cage. Bun was a glorious rabbit, huge, red-furred, elegant, and terribly tame. She came to the doorstep when we called, like a dog. Quite by chance our dwarf male, Chipper, escaped one day, and they did what rabbits do best. By October, we had barn bunnies. We kept Sticky Bun, Wally and Crow from that litter. They lived fancy free, in and around the barn, and we relied on their daily travels from barn to house to keep us entertained. Before Wally was castrated, however, there were more bunnies. From Sticky Bun's litter we captured Sparky and Pignut and assigned them to cages.

But Sparky especially hated the cage, so last November, with the skills of my veterinarian sister put to work on the kitchen table, we castrated Sparky and turned him loose, too.

The rabbits loved their days here. Summers, we sat on the porch and watched them, digging in the June petunia patch, skipping down the lane in the July dusk, lying spread eagle in the August sunshine.

And then came this October, the seventh since Sticky was born. One day she was no longer at the small coop where I feed the rabbits at night. Sparky was absent the next day. About that time we found wads of white fluffy fur at the edge of the forest, all that was left of Sparky.

The predator picked off Wally and then Crow within the next two days — four rabbits within one week, after years of frolic. Pignut, carefully housed in a new cage, a birthday present from Arek, for the first time ever seemed happy to be the only confined creature.

We knew there were skunks around, but those benign animals slept at times inside the chicken coop, taking only an egg or a mouse. Raccoon scat appeared in the front yard, but raccoons seem to lack the agility required to catch rabbits. A fox? A weasel? There is a hawk about, but the rabbits disappeared at night.

Last fall, the hawk, however, worked his damage, snatching the most elegant of our golden roosters from the front yard flock of 32 bantams, like a frog snagging a fly. My husband opened the door to find the hawk on the doorstep tearing Pumpkin apart feather by feather. Since then 14 more chickens bit the dust; luckily they were replaced by 26 newly-hatched chicks in August. But the hawk is back again — a sharp-shinned? a broad-winged? Both are around, but I've been so startled I've never looked closely. We caught him red-handed, with his claws in Mrs. Dash's back. That time I scared him off before he could lift off with her and she survived, minus a sackful of feathers.

But it isn't over. Two other golden roosters are gone now, and two new chicks. That hawk is having Thanksgiving dinner daily. The only roosters who survive today are Little Leaf and Dusty. The irony of it all centers on Dusty, who is an old, old rooster, chased from the little coop by the golden roosters. In order to survive, Dusty took up residence in our garage attic. Each evening when all the other bantams head to their coop, Dusty ambles into the garage and hops up the stairs to his solitary perch. His isolation may be his salvation.

But the bantam and bunny stories aren't the worst. At the big barn we house our egg-layers. They are free range chickens, who have hatched young ones, too, this summer, and who roost where they please in the sheep barn at night. These chickens are big and mighty, small turkey-size almost. A hawk is no match for them. Something clever and strong must capture these chickens. This flock included roosters, eight or so, and more than twenty hens, some with chicks.

The barn predator has depleted that bunch. They now number three hens and four chicks. Overnight, the barn grew quiet. No longer is the voice of the rooster heard at dawn.

Perhaps the drought is at fault. Our neighbor talks about the increased visibility and evidence of wild creatures venturing closer to homes. An increase of squirrel road kill is reported, the cause attributable to their search for water sources, often near human habitation. Food sources are more scarce — berries, nuts, and fruit smaller or absent due to the lack of water.

Perhaps our neighbor is right about conditions, but this is little consolation to us. For ten years we have not caged our small animals. Now it seems that we must for their safety and survival. All this carnage doesn't make me like October any better.

Gone unnoticed
December, 1995

He followed the same trail the man who owns the land walks regularly. It was easier that way, on a packed footpath, with no icy edges of snow to pull at his feet as he broke through the delicate crust of snow. Darkness covered his passage. His scat, dropped where the man had opened a gate in the stone wall, revealed his presence; otherwise, he would have gone unnoticed.

Except — after darkness had sealed and locked the world for another bitter night, the young boy paused in his evening chores and heard his eerie, ghostly call at a distance.

"Mom," he said later that evening, while we sat snug and safe at the kitchen table, pasta steaming before us and the wood stove puffing away, "I heard a coyote. Weird. After he stopped, all the neighborhood dogs began barking, almost frantically." I shivered, not in fear, but out of a deeper respect for a world I have absolutely no control over.

"Are the sheep all in the paddock?" My first question. And after that is answered there is no other protection against a natural world that I cannot see and only know from signs. A secret, hidden world of animals exists in close proximity to our daily lives, and yet I know little about it. I wish I could stay awake all night, hide myself in a tree, and just watch the fields around me for ten hours when the invisible become real, no longer spirits that pass in the dark.

I have become accustomed to the existence and interaction with the obvious animals — like squirrels, mice, and meadow voles. This summer, chipmunks renewed their acquaintance, thanks largely to the death of our old cat, who abhorred vegetarian meals and dined nightly on small rodents, leaving gall bladders as evidence of a successful hunt. Without Pippin's presence, the chipmunks rebounded.

There are birds, too, who connect me to a world beyond human interaction, often providing the link to a spiritual essence. I have walked land and forest, stood at ocean's edge or river's shore with the most special people I know, and marveled at the antics and colors and behaviors of birds. But birds are easy to observe, if I take the time. After my father's death, sitting alone at the edge of

Lake St. George, I watched his spirit move when out of the darkness one lone wood duck appeared, swam towards me, the ebony lake water following behind him like a welcoming path to somewhere. As he neared the shore, with one short cry he bid goodbye and flew north into the blackness.

But I am perplexed by the lives of creatures I observe as if through a veil and only for a moment, and whose behaviors and identities I have not studied as methodically as I have those of birds. With that thought, on a snow-covered morning as more and more flakes fell and bound us closer to the house and human interactions, I was startled to find a message on the kitchen counter. "Mom, I found this." The arrow pointed to a picture in an opened field guide, a shorttail weasel, *Mustela erminea*.

Later Arek was to retell his encounter at dawn, cup of coffee clutched in his hands, sleepy eyes barely open, as he peered out the west window. At the base of the house from a pile of rock emerged the weasel's head. "Like a snake, he slithered, flattened, over the rocks, covering them as if his body were liquid white fur."

As quickly as he appeared, he was gone, gliding into a break in the stone wall like quicksilver, only to reappear at the end of the wall where he turned and vanished below the creek bank. His fur, already white for winter, concealed him at dawn.

How long has he been living here? How much benefit has he brought to our community? The red squirrel population is exploding. Will this weasel grow fat dining on red squirrel, or has he already been responsible for the chicken coop carnage?

The signs of wild animals continually remind me of the winter stories of Swedish tomtens whose footprints alone mark nighttime journeys from shed to barn to forest. The tomtens of Maine forests are mysterious, too. A feather, a call, a track, a glimpse — solitary hints provide a fleeting look into lives that parallel ours. The sharp-shinned hawk perching near the bantams' feeding tray, the shrike trapping a chickadee on the front porch, the barred owl calling in the shadows, targeting our rabbits, the weasel and the coyote arriving in the night — these lives all exist near ours, but clandestinely, leave only a mark to attest to their passing.

Titans of the forest
January, 1996

Trees are like the dinosaurs of the plant world but not in the sense of being extinct. It is the size that counts. They easily top Tyrannosaurus Rex — in sound, as well as height. I never look up enough when I am outside to truly appreciate the dinosaur-like plants that tower over me. Rather, my view is usually straight on, about six feet above ground level. In spring, in autumn, after a snowstorm, I see this picture: lacy, delicate trees, etched and painted by Mother Nature. I forget there is another — the view of giants.

In the middle of a snow-sleet storm this past week, Nell, our new pup, and I went for a walk with the wind swirling around us, tugging at her fur and my scarf, bringing tears to our eyes. There were no other distractions in this storm, only the elements and us. Near the ice pond we stopped for a while, stood still. Nell leaned against my leg as we were engulfed by the rage of the wind. Twigs and small branches flew through the air in a fury. Detritus from last autumn's leaf fall was scooped up and hurled back to earth. Wind howled, and the trees above us answered in kind. They were not taking this beating like lambs.

Ice-covered branches and the slender tip tops of trees clinked together, jostling each other like fans at a football game. They pushed and shoved under the wind's influence, always returning to their original position and then moving quickly in the opposite direction, all the while chattering and clanging. Ice in a glass. Tap dancers on stage. Horses on parade with their clattering shoes hitting asphalt. All of those sounds rained down upon Nell and me as we stood under the bare ash tree towering 50 feet above us. I crouched beside her, held onto her for comfort. The forest was filled with passions in a storm, and nowhere was it more violent than under the trees.

The more the wind pushed, the more the trunks swayed, groaning as if sick or injured, left to die along a path. Unlike their distant branches that reach the sky and greet the sun on brighter days, the trunks sustain the weight of the entire tree, limb to branch to stem to leaf. Theirs is the task of transporting food, minerals, and water. Here the sap swells, rises, freezes, and then slowly melts. Here the transportation system — switching terminals, platforms, and connections — carries out its work. It is a life of burden and responsibility — and endurance.

On the first farm by the ocean where we once lived, when my children were young and I was frequently awake in the dark, bewitching hours of night with a baby on my shoulder, I would watch the white pine and northern red oak along the shore. Throughout winter those trees moved like tyrannosaurs stalking along the ocean's edge. Their entire bodies seemed in action except for their feet which were rooted and solid, the support that kept them from tumbling. Groaning, not from illness, but from exertion in the battle, the trees struggled to remain upright.

I am fascinated when trees have lost that battle, when I come upon the newly-split wood, splintered into daggers, of a fallen pine deep in a forest. The intricate web of roots and rootlets that have provided water and minerals, sustained a tree for a lifetime, are exposed. Death of a titan is dramatic. Sixty feet of fallen tree is not to be scoffed at.

At the university in Ohio where I went to school, an old red oak that once defined the center of the campus, now over 200 years old, was taken down this year. It did not lose a battle to a wind storm as the trees in my woods may, but fear of the consequences of such a defeat drove the campus officials to "remove" the tree first. Their comment, "It was only a matter of time before a storm blew it over…"

But just imagine. Sprouted about 1795, that red oak grew up in a forest which stretched from Lake Erie to the Ohio River. It watched over the birth of the university and the comings and goings of countless students who strolled beneath its branches. People do not take kindly to the loss of such a tree.

I wonder, then, about the lesser-known trees that tower over Nell and me, the ones complaining loudly about the strength of this particular storm. They will survive. They are still young in tree years and have flexible trunks and tenacious roots. Long after we have gone on our way, these ash and maple, hemlock and fir, pine and beech which inhabit our woods will have withstood the sting of sleet, the weight of snow, the pelting of rain. The titans of this forest may wail in response to the wind, but they will win the battle. From the viewpoint of giants there is no room for whimperers. Nell and I will do best to weather this storm under the protection of a roof.

Life seen from a new angle
March, 1996

The gray goose flew away last Tuesday, just before the snow melted. She was standing in the far southeast pasture. Imprisoned by three electric fences, one inside the other inside the other, she was like a child's toy, hidden in the innermost box — except I could see her from the road on my way home from work. Her plaintive cry hung just below the tree tops.

Never, in ten years, has a goose on our farm traveled to that distant pasture. I could not imagine how she waddled, struggling through snow and wire fencing to reach the high point, where she stood as a sentinel now, raising her head and honking to the metallic sky, a lone trumpeter after the gig was over.

I came inside, changed clothes. "I'm going to the pasture to retrieve the goose," I said to no one in particular.

We don't usually go to the southeast pasture in winter except to cut our Christmas tree. It is off limits, inaccessible once the snow accumulates to any depth. *How* did that goose get here, I wondered, as I trudged along the edge of the stream that runs through the lower end of the pasture. At least the advent of spring thaw had melted the snow enough along the stream's edge so that walking was not difficult, but I could see no goose footprints to indicate that she had taken this same path.

I wanted to herd her back toward the house, assuming she would then take the lane to the barn, the route she and her white goose companion strolled every day. I was certain she would recognize her location and go "home." I rounded up on her, feeling a lot like a sheep dog instinctively pushing the flock. She turned in the exact direction I wanted her to go and began uttering one sad sound, a repetitive quarter note somewhere around low E. "Onk, onk, onk, onk," she whispered.

Then she zigzagged, quickly, back in the direction we had just come. The ground I had gained she had just retaken and she was back where she started.

So we began again. In the middle of the field I was playing "fox and geese," the children's snow game, only this time with a real goose. And the tables were turning; she was winning.

As the game went on, the question of how *this* goose arrived in *this* field, increasingly nagged at me. The entire blanket of white to the north and west, the direction of house and barn, was pristine, an unblemished stretch of snow. As the goose circled back and I, now the fox and no longer a sheep dog, tried another maneuver, I stumbled across the answer. To the south, from the large stand of hemlock, spruce, and fir was a perfectly traced trail — palm-sized, web-shaped footprints, one after another in a flawless unswerving line from woods to the center of the pasture. How in heaven's name did this goose get to the woods first?

That question was no sooner in my head than it was answered. The gray goose stretched her huge wings, wings that on a previous occasion had bloodied my nose when I tried to remove her from a nest. Now those same powerful wings were beating at the ground, stirring up snow. She began to run, the pounding wings propelling her forward more rapidly than I could move. I was dumbfounded.

We have had maybe ten geese in our 25 years of farming. Geese live a long time. The gray goose herself is almost ten and the white goose she left behind is older than that. In all those years I have seen these fowl fight off foxes (real ones) and attack meter-reader men (who beat hasty retreats to the safety of pickup trucks); they intimidate all small children and dogs; when they are sitting on eggs, no one, not even the farmer approaches them (consequence: bloody nose). Yet, I had never seen them fly.

Until now. The gray goose flap-ran another fifteen feet and lifted off, low-slung like a cargo plane, but banking precisely and swiftly like a fighter jet. She rose so sharply that it was not a problem at all to clear the tallest spruce for she was heading south, far away from the barn and me. Within seconds she had disappeared from my sight.

I stood alone in the middle of the rather dreary-looking field. It was March, a bedraggled, lonely month. I felt bereft and quite a bit cheated. What had she heard that I had not? Whose call or what instinct stirred her, after ten years, to leave home? Why had she never flown before and then in the blink of an eye, soared fifty feet above my head? Imagine what it must be like to be transported — to really see life from a new angle.

Meanwhile, back in the barn, in a familiar corner, the white goose continues laying her eggs.

Nell
April, 1996

In between snowstorms this month, Nellie and I have had a chance for a good walk or two — not that there is much greenery to see yet, but it won't be long, and I keep telling her she'll like spring as much as she has loved winter. Nellie is new to the world and hasn't been around for a full circle of the sun yet.

Snow appears to Nellie like a gift from the gods. If ever a dog matched a season it is Nell and winter. We have had a young polar bear living with us for months, one who greeted each new snowfall with euphoria. But now the weather is changing and she has discovered some dislikes — too much water and the sound of wind are unsettling to her.

She does pay attention to the birds, though. Every new springtime arrival this week merited careful study. She is quite a listener, and all play and nonsense stop when a new sound is on the air. Red-winged blackbirds, birds whose song might pass for a gurgle from a kitchen drain, have fascinated her. But then, so have the ponderous, mellow mourning doves who peer at her from the top of the feeding station.

Nell arrived December 29, courtesy of my veterinarian sister, tucked in the back of an airline traveling case. She refused to come out of her cage, hesitant and timid, cuddled into her blue blanket. She stayed in the cage for nine hours, looking like, well, a Christmas angel — white all over except for a dusting of honey-color on her back, a beatific attitude, gentle manners, and a look on her face that would melt the hardest of hearts.

My sister had said, "She's a bit shy, so be sure and socialize her. She's used to being in a barn." So we starting socializing, with my dear 80 year-old mother hand feeding her because "I don't think Nellie likes to eat from a dish."

Nellie eats from a dish just fine these days, weighing over 70 pounds and not yet out of puppyhood. Raised as her ancestors were to guard homesteads, hike mountains, herd sheep, and survive great long winters, she fits that mold. This month of April has been right up her genetic alley. Just when it looked like all the snow was gone, the one-two punch hit again... and again... much to Nellie's delight.

She tugs the twig arms out of my snowman and eats them, then chews the pompom off the snowman's hat. She goes to the barn and frolics in the hay, teases the sheep, rolls in the snowdrifts, and sniffs the perimeter for predator smells. She tunnels through the snow in the garden and finds a hollow shell of a squash, which keeps her entertained for hours. She sneaks into the chicken coop, scrambling under the barrier meant to keep her out, just so she can steal eggs. She chases red squirrels, bats her own tennis ball through the slush in the driveway, hangs on the rope swing; one day I expect to see her sailing high into the air. When she tires of simple play, she sleeps on the front step. Her duty is to survey her domain, and she instinctively knows that.

But on days when the snow is melting, like today, she looks to me for entertainment.

Can you imagine loving winter for winter's sake, so that all else would not matter, that a season alone could provide happiness and delight? There's a message there, I'm sure, and a lesson to be learned, but somehow it is lost on me, as I eagerly await the emergence of the first red trillium.

Nell doesn't know that yet, so together we padded along the forest trail to the bittersweet-blackberry patch. We stopped first at the ice pond, which had a thin layer of slush still coating the center. (That night we were to hear the wood frogs.) We went through the patch and out to an open field, Nellie at my heels, looking left and right. This stuff was new. Yes, she had traveled it for four months, over snow though, her ancestral landscape. Dried leaves and dead grass represented new territory.

Nothing green was emerging anywhere, and I was discouraged. We headed west toward the spot where an old stone wall intersects with a giant white pine, one with limbs that looks as if she has more arms than Medusa had hair. Near that juncture is a swale, the one spot with promise and the youthful feel of spring. Water ran everywhere and green mosses slurped readily. Nellie, pausing, for she doesn't like to get wet, ventured into the swale off the path. Twice she went in, but each time came back out to stand and listen intently, peering toward the north. She stared often and long enough to make me uneasy. What did she hear that I couldn't? Her sound-sense can be spooky.

Finally, I coaxed her out of the water and we started up the hill toward the Medusa-tree. At that moment, a ruffed grouse exploded from the bushes beside the path, setting my heart racing. Nellie had an I-told-you-so look on her face. She does hear far beyond my capacity.

That's what makes me think she's "just gonna love spring" as much as winter. If ever there were a season for sounds this one is it. Nell, I tell her... just you wait.

I know where the red trillium grow
May, 1996

Shakespeare's Oberon may "know a bank where the wild thyme blows, where oxlips and the nodding violet grows," but I bet I know a better one. Today I found a whole roadside where red trillium grow. And mixed right in with those nodding heads of purple-red "wake-robins" are the delicate flowers of bellwort whose yellow color is as creamy as butter. If that isn't enough to excite all of Shakespeare's fairies celebrating spring, I don't know what it would take.

It surely helped me perk right up. Disgruntled because of the lack of opportunities to go birding — too cold, too rainy, too early (and now I am worried that it will soon be too late as daily the leaves loom larger at my window) — two of us set off for a walk. I wore mittens, mind you, in the middle of May! But in spite of the briskness of the temperature, the beauty of my favorite month was not to be ignored. April showers have truly brought May flowers, even if the warblers aren't here yet. Often I overlook the tiny blossoms in my headlong rush to catch the first oriole, snag that first sighting of a hummingbird, snap up the first parula.

The beauty of "flower watching" lies in its ease. No cumbersome binoculars to fuss with, no careful movements so as not to frighten a hermit thrush. Just walk right up to these flowering creatures and touch them if you wish. They don't scare easily or flit behind a spruce trunk.

The red trillium covered a football field's distance along an old stone wall. Since that wall was built, mountains of soil have been heaved up around the rocks and, in this cluttering, trillium and bellwort have taken hold. Tucked in between them are the unfolding heads of ferns. The large clumped groups, mostly cinnamon and interrupted ferns, stand tall, facing each other like a crowd of guests at a cocktail party snubbing the uninvited. For those unwanted lady ferns, there is nothing left to do except gracefully dance alone in the wind, moving between and filling all the spaces around the clumped ferns. It is here that the trillium, bellwort, and an occasional purple wood violet add their color to a sea of green.

Across the road where the bank slopes away, we looked down upon a carpet of candy cane-like wood anemones. I scrambled down the bank, touching the unopened pink blossom of one plant. Much as I love chasing chestnut-sided warblers, I could never inspect that bird as closely as I could these anemones. As far as the eye could see, anemones decorated the forest floor. Tucked in here, too, were the ubiquitous wild lily-of-the-valley. Only one or two had sent up their flower spikes, but the single green leaves, rich with all this rain, covered all the ground not belonging to the anemones. I wonder if flowers have range wars. This side is mine. This is yours. Do they fight to take over each other's territories like the red-winged blackbirds do?

I wanted to find trailing arbutus. It has been years since I found a bank where those flowers grow. Arbutus were always May basket flowers to me. Years ago, when our children were small, my friend Pat and her children faithfully delivered tiny baskets on May first. In them were violets and dandelions, candy kisses, a balloon, a new pencil, and always a sprig of trailing arbutus. I wish I could find those flowers of spring again.

Back at home, near the pasture, we found patches of purple wood violets, spreading white blossoms of wild strawberries, and out where the sheep will soon graze, the ground is white with the profusion of bluets, Quaker ladies, spring's gracious welcomers. Shakespeare's fairies must prepare the bower, fill it with these flowers on my hill and roadside, and get ready to welcome this month of May.

I had not wanted to go outside, but now I was glad for the adventure. Now — nothing is left but to await the arrival of the birds. As I thought that, standing in the front yard, the pileated woodpecker and his mate flew into the ash tree by the newly-leafed lilac bush. Aha. Surely the wood thrush and blue-headed vireo are close behind. May will be perfect.

The moon plays games
October, 1996

October is a study in contrasts. This morning at dawn, fall's still life was breathtakingly beautiful. Time, and the work of Jack Frost, had cast a spell, an immobilizing, ethereal enchantment that froze the landscapes on canvases. Field after field is painted in the same manner with brilliant leaves, their colors smeared and dabbed, providing the background for the picture. In front of each gathering of trees graze the farm animals, silently, peacefully. Above the entire scene hangs the moon, a silver dollar, a translucent shimmering child's ball, fighting to keep its sway over the encroaching rays of the sun.

A competition is at hand between sun and moon. Down the road at our neighbor's house, the sheep stand against the rising sun in silhouette, heads bent to the ground, the line of each sheep's back making an arch from tail to nose. Fleece shines with frost drops changing to dew, each melting under warmth as the sun scales the tops of the trees.

Around the corner, at another small farm, the same scene repeats itself. This time, the animal is chestnut, dark and silky, a study in the art of using the color brown. The horse, like the sheep, stands in stillness, but now, with my back to the sun, I can see her colors clearly, watch her eyelids flicker, hear her soft snorts disturbing the morning air around her. The sheep have been only outlines. The horse is a perfect corporeal image.

The moon seems to be following me. I can never get my bearings about the moon at dawn. She is a slippery thing, going where she pleases and not following any laws of Mother Nature. On down the road, with the moon running from the sun which follows my footsteps, the two of us together pass a garden long gone to bed. The farmer here has cleaned away all the debris of once-productive tomato and squash vines. The moon laughs at the damage done under her watchful eye. In fall she plays games like this. Now only the skeletons of corn plants remain, the unnecessary sentinels, guarding the soil perhaps, for there is nothing left for even a raccoon to steal.

Nearer the town, before the hubbub of traffic and work schedules fill the air, the last farm appears and Jack Frost again paints the picture of color and farm animals. Fifty magnificent brown and white cows dapple the still-green fields. These meadows lead to the river's edge. Here the warmth of water meets the brisk snap of air. Fog rises, just as the sun, creating an eerie, yet slightly welcoming feeling to the day. Little wisps of haze obscure one cow as another emerges into sunlight. A carnival of mirrors is at work here. Mist and cows and sun. The moon, suddenly, seems to have permitted the sun to rule for the day, biding her own time until darkness, moon's domain, arrives again.

For it is the moon better than any other natural object that provides the point of stark contrasts for autumn. The differences become painfully evident when night falls and the moon rises. This object hovering at the horizon is not the silvery plaything of dawn, the gleaming fox about to slip away for the day after raiding the last of the chicken coop. No indeed. The moon of October's night is the dark gold of a pirate's treasure, the strong, powerful gleam of frost and shadows, of things slightly fearful and foreboding.

Days shorten dramatically in fall and power returns to the moon. With it, farm animals and gentle pastoral scenes are gone. The picture becomes one of the night creatures. This is the time of bats. In the purple dusk, even before the sheep have bedded down and before hibernation urges set in, a large chunky bat has circled our house on a regular run. This is his hour. Snatch the last of the moths who hover around the porch light. Grab the few remaining insects on the wing.

Night in autumn tastes of Halloween. The crunch of footsteps on the dying maple and ash leaves, a pleasant sound in daylight, is unnerving at night. "Who goes there?" I wonder. Only the cats who prowl and waltz in the light of the reigning moon, for they are enchanted. Two calico cats, tails twitching, stealthily maneuver around the edge of the early darkness. The wild creatures of the night watch in awe. The owl, the fox, the skunk, the deer, the porcupine. They are all out there somewhere, wearing the magic of fall on their coats as they prepare for winter.

As November arrives and deepens, the transition will be complete. The last days of Indian summer will dwindle. Nights will be cold and hard with frost. The ground will thicken and hold hoof prints. Skim ice will form on the ponds. The farm geese will no longer swim at dawn nor porcupines drink at dark.

But for a few days more, fall's contrasts continue. Mist in the morning gives way to sunshine. Fog at dusk shrouds the magical shadows of the moon.

Huck comes out of hibernation
February, 1997

The cat is a walking lightning bolt, so full of static electricity that I am afraid she will damage my computer when she rubs up against the monitor before she steps nimbly over the keyboard and snuggles into my lap. That's a condition of these dry winter days. I wish she would just go back to hibernating and stop shocking me. But the truth is the days are getting longer and the sap is beginning to stir in cats as much as in the maple trees. It must surely be that extra jolt of sunshine streaming in the bedroom window that is arousing her.

Huckleberry Pie is the second best cat we have ever had. She's 17 years old now and still going strong, except for her daily pill of Tapazole which keeps her thyroid in line. She's a little thinner than I would like and her eating habits have, from my point of view, deteriorated rapidly. From her point of view they have become refined, high-class. Cooked meat from the human table is her preference these days, with salmon and baked chicken among the extravagant choices. Facing starvation, she will resort to a few bites of dry food and an occasional tiny can of expensive cat pâté, but generally she holds out until I begin to worry and share my dinner. Chili and vegetable soup (homemade only) are also high on her list, as is licking a stick of butter.

But Huckle is best known around here for something other than her finicky eating habits and it isn't for her cute little pink nose — placed in the middle of that calico face which is orange on one side and black on the other. Nor is she famous for the length of her whiskers which stretch four long inches or for her pristine clean white paws. Much as I love her, she is not famous for curling next to my pillow at night and purring for hours, telling the story of her contentment with life on the farm.

Her reputation lies in the exercise of unbridled power. She is the hunter, hiding behind a facade of ladylike features and delicate bones. As the evenings have warmed slightly, Huck has ventured outside again, flexing her muscles, sharpening her claws against the still-frozen ash tree beside the deck. No creature was safe if Huck, in her younger days, was in the mood. I locked her in the house for one entire month when the bluebirds were fledging, but her favorite quarry has always been the unsuspecting mammal.

Once again, she was finicky in her selection, never dining on ordinary field mice or voles. Those she left for Pippin, her mother. Huckle's reputation in the little mammal kingdom was that of a squirrel killer. Tales abounded of her ferocity and tails of gray squirrels appeared regularly on the front steps. Huckle is not a vegetarian in spite of her affinity for vegetable soup (homemade).

Once I came upon her in the act of killing the red squirrel who had tormented us for months at the bird feeder. She bided her time, pretending to snooze among the daylilies, but her eyes never closed. One day, zap. The squirrel was in her claws and sweet ladylike Huckleberry Pie was transformed into the power-hungry Sylvester Stallone of the feline world. The red squirrel didn't have a chance, his dying screams a match for the shrieks of horror movies.

Her best conquest, and one I have not seen matched yet, was the systematic beheading of the weasel who came to prey on the chicken coop. The weasel, a tiny shorttail, was decapitated in the garage. It was a neat job, with almost no blood to mess up the premises. The head lay by the doorstep, the body next to the car, a scene for the mystery writer. The only clue to the identity of the villain was that Huckle reeked of weasel musk for a week.

She exercised her power trip prerogative this December when Frank, a smart aleck youngster from the streets of Philadelphia, came to visit. Frank lives in a college apartment and struts his stuff regularly as he growls at birds and alley cat types who skit past his window. For fun, he beats up a stuffed monkey. He thought he was one tough cat until he ran into the likes of an outraged Huckle determined to defend her turf.

We locked Frank in a bedroom and tacked a blanket over a small entrance into the room from the attic loft. Five minutes after Huck realized Frank was in the house, the caterwauling echoed through the halls. Poor Frank, pummeled and defeated, huddled under the bed. For a week Huckle found her way into the bedroom and clobbered Frank daily. Finally, we boarded up the little doorway with a huge piece of plywood.

Frank made only one other mistake. When I accidentally left the door open, he rushed out into the world of the "rest of the house." Before long, he had discovered the Christmas tree where Huckle discovered him and proceeded to destroy the train set, the manger scene, beating Frank to a pulp. Frank left in January. We heard through the grape vine that he is just now regaining his previous machismo.

But other than the Frank episode, Huckle's exercise of power has slowed this past year. Her hearing is no longer acute. Age is taking its toll. I haven't seen a squirrel tail in months. The outdoors may be too cold for an old cat. Or maybe not. Maybe I am underestimating her, for she has not abandoned the hunter role entirely.

To keep herself in shape, she regularly targets our dog. Nellie (at 113 pounds) puts up a good show, prancing in front of the eight pound cat, shadowing her around the house, but whenever Huck spins around and takes a stand, Nell simply slumps to the floor, puts her nose in her paws and stares into Huckle's hunter eyes. Huck hisses once, to impress Nell with the seriousness of the situation, and then sits like an Egyptian cat with multiple secrets to take to the pyramid. Nell better watch out. (Remember Frank?) Huckle likes big meat and it is almost spring. She may be working up an appetite.

A city cat comes to stay
June, 1997

Jillian and Aaron, her future husband, city folk for now, came to stay a while this month, all eager to enjoy Maine, and Frank returned with them. In fact, Frank came to stay for the summer. After his owners departed, leaving us the caretakers of a cranky, housebound, energetic tornado (who also fought daily with our cat), I slid open the kitchen screen door and booted Frank out.

Life hasn't been the same since. The first few days of June, Frank was like a schoolboy newly released from the confines of the classroom, not quite sure what to make of the world waiting out there, a little uncertain in an unfamiliar world of freedom. But, like this month's rush into hot weather, Frank was soon slipping into country ways as if he had been born and bred to rural life.

Fluttering tiger swallowtails captured his fancy. He could dance with them daily in the front yard and zip under the late blooming tulips where the hummingbird hovered. He was cautious though and not one to capture any wild creatures. It was thrill enough just to watch. The excitement of green grass, real grass, coaxed him into wandering farther from the house until he discovered trees. Frank had stumbled upon the ultimate jungle gym. Up he went, thirty feet running straight on the side of the ash tree. Down he came, head first, on a suicide run. He survived, the terror of the roller coaster's descent overcome by the desire to shoot up the next tree in the yard. Frank entertained himself for hours playing hot wheels, with the maple and ash trees as his personal tracks.

A few nights later, my nieces were in the back yard playing frisbee with Nellie. By dark, when the playing field was filled with the festival of lightning bugs, Frank joined in, outwitting even the fastest human runner. Frank had learned how to play tag in the city apartment and frisbee seemed like that game, just a lot more fun.

And then he discovered the barn.

It was here that he had seen Nellie, the polar-bear type dog who is supposed to herd sheep, make her daily forays, but his courage to venture that far was a bit long in coming. Once, however, Frank located the goose and ducks, life changed all over again. Here were pinwheels in a flurry, running, honking, flapping, quacking. Frank realized that he could set the whole carnival in motion himself, just by chasing. He had seen Nellie herd sheep. Her approach was haphazard, whatever suited her at the moment. She would desert her napping spot on the cool garage floor and round up the loose sheep when she was good and ready. Frank's attitude was different. After all, he was a can-do cat from the mean city streets. He wanted action now.

So the goose got it. Frank started herding her, up the driveway, down the driveway. The poor goose. Life was getting quite difficult. The male duck also chased the goose. Her options for escape were limited as Frank joined forces with the white duck to run the goose ragged. It was fun while it lasted. The goose, after 14 years spent waddling on the farm, started low-level flying, and Frank was no match for air travel. He resorted to something easier to chase — the sheep.

The sheep were breaking out of their new pasture daily, so Nellie had been getting hourly instructions to go "get the sheep," a command which interrupted her sleep on that cool garage floor. She wasn't quick to respond, often looking at us as if to say, "Go get them yourself." Frank stepped in to fill the lag time it took for Nell to get around to business.

The last time I went to the pond to round up Sprout and her lamb, I called Nellie. Frank showed up instead, hopping, skipping, chomping at the proverbial bit, inquiring when were we going to get on with the exercise of ordering the sheep around. It was a near disaster, with the sheep finally trotting down the road, heading to town, but at least Frank tried. And he didn't give up. The next night at dinner, we looked out the window to see five sheep streaking across the front lawn.

"Yep, Nellie's finally doing her job."

Not quite. Close on the heels of the last-in-line sheep, snarling like a fierce mountain lion, was Frank, the fresh air cat.

"Yep, Frank's doing his job."

I am not sure if he'll keep up the labor. Later that day, on another herding run, I saw a ewe stop in her tracks, turn around and whop Frank a good one with her head. Stunned momentarily, he tumbled into the creek, but didn't stay long. The last I saw him he was back up the apple tree peering down on the red squirrel in the feeder. Fat chance this guy will return to D.C. in the fall. I think he's city folk come to stay.

I hate the tractor
September, 1997

Every year the same thing happens as summer rushes toward its conclusion. The hay is never all cut and all the "helpers" seem to have evaporated, gone to work or college. Pete, with a glum look, says, "Don't worry. I can bale and then pick up by myself..." His meaning hangs heavy. I know it is much more work for him alone. And so, grudgingly, I offer to drive the baler. "You sure?" he asks. What am I to say?

So here I am, sitting behind the 38 horse engine of the yellow and green John Deere, encased by a wall of glass and steel which captures all the heat the motor generates and blasts it into my face. I hate driving the baler. I don't like the John Deere much better. That heat is just one reason.

I hate it for a lot of reasons. The second is I can never remember from one year to the next how to put it in gear. This tractor (unlike the gray Ford which our kindly next-door neighbor loans us on a regular basis — I love the Ford) has two gear shifts for getting the machine moving. One has numbers like I and II and the letter P inside a box on it and other stuff I have no idea about. The second gear shift has double numbers, like 1-5 and 3-7. Who knows what that means? With the Ford, I just push the gear shift and it goes. With the John Deere I can have one gear shift in-gear and one out-of-gear and still take the clutch out and it won't stall. It makes no sense.

But the gear shifts aren't the problem as much as my husband is. He thinks I know what to do with them and then tries not to act exasperated when I ask, "How do I put it in reverse?"

The third reason I hate driving the baler is I always get the hay jammed into the big feeding maw of the baler itself. Pete grumps as he jumps off the hay wagon, yells at me to put it in neutral, and shouts, "Don't turn off the PTO." (Well, that's another thing I hate, the PTO. I want to turn it off every time I stop because of all those horror stories I read in *Farm Journal* about farmers losing limbs to machines without automatic PTO shut off.) But my husband says I have to stop it at a certain spot and I never get that right and then he has to turn the fly wheel "that's got the centrifugal force, blah, blah, higher rpms to keep it turning, blah, blah..." all stuff I don't get — and it is always a mess until the baler gets unjammed and we get this whole dog and pony show on the road again. I wonder if about now he is thinking it isn't worth having me along to ease the pain of end-of-the-season haying.

The fourth reason I hate driving the baler is steep inclines. With the little Ford, I can rake hay to my heart's content. (Now, *that* I love, raking hay. With the Ford, which has no roof or window, I can see blue sky and sunshine and fritillary butterflies for miles.) And only once did I get going down a hill too fast. I panicked and put the clutch in only to go even faster, a bit out of control. With the John Deere and the baler behind, even a slight incline makes me feel like I am tipping over. I stand up with my foot on the brake, like I'm riding a horse down a hill, and push against the momentum of the tractor. When I have reached the point of absolute assurance that I am flipping over in a second, I desert the row I am baling, moving to a flatter level. Later that day, my husband goes back and bales those rows alone.

But the worst part of all of this is that, when I am driving the baler, with so much noise, I have to pay attention: one, to where the front wheels and the rear wheels are lined up; two, to the hay rows and the baler's speed of processing hay; three, to the position of the fly wheel; four, to the instructions from my husband; and then, because he really is a good guy, and I want to make sure he doesn't lose his balance on the wagon, I must pay attention to my starts and stops — so much paying attention that I can't watch the world around me which is really what I want to be doing in September.

Like — in the pond the other day, I was floating, counting frogs all by myself. No one was there to tell me what to do, and I watched a dragonfly drink. He hovered and then splashed into the water quickly. Before I could even focus, he was hovering again. Up and down. Up and down. Ripples in concentric circles dissipated from the spot where the dragonfly hit the water. For just a moment I was an insect.

Like — this morning I was alone in the front yard when rustling bushes along the stone wall caught my eye. On a windless day they jiggled and shook. I investigated. A robin, jumping like he was on a trampoline, shot straight up and snatched a blackberry, tumbled back to the ground, and jumped again. Another jump. Another berry. Another tumble. A bird's world.

Like — the goldfinch drinking from the dog's dish in the back yard. The monarch, the first of the season, floating. The cricket scurrying. The ant with a half eaten white lacy moth in his mouth, hustling along the front porch bricks. The bumblebee laden with pollen caught in the morning glory blossom. That's what I want to do in September — pay attention.

Last night Lynn and Eric, our neighbors, came over. She had been helping him bale the last of their summer's hay, too. But, Lynn doesn't drive their tractor, a David Brown. Eric gets to do that — sit back, laze along, one arm on the steering wheel, one on the fender of the tire. Her job is to pick up each bale and stack it on the hay wagon! I just shut my mouth. I'll gladly drive and watch bugs and birds some other day.

Mushrooms, bats, and Poe
October, 1997

They popped up in the front yard over night. Yesterday the lawn was green and rolling, inviting as an Indian summer afternoon. The sun washed the tips of the grass blades; the air was bright and alive with agitated flying insects. Yet there was a lazy atmosphere to the whole scene as well. A silence descended as the bugs danced to soundless music.

Book IV: Truths

While this bucolic scene occurred above ground, underground a sinister scene was creeping along in the endless darkness. Following a plot from Edgar Allen Poe, threads of the genus *boletaceae*, a type of basidiomycete, were about to make their ominous fruiting bodies known. These threads, as they grew, created fiber networks which formed the mycelium. At dawn they erupted. The scene changed.

The setting could have been for "The Fall of the House of Usher." Poe warned of a dull, dark, and soundless day in the autumn of the year. Well, it occurred before my very eyes. Scattered under the ash trees like shattered fragments of the house of Usher itself were plate-sized mushrooms — not the cute little mushrooms seen in children's fairy books where red-capped little gnomes smoke pipes beneath the white spreading gills. My lawn was dressed with ugly, big, brown ones. And these boletes were not the colors of a mellow brown — cinnamon, sable, chocolate. My crop decayed into rotten-flesh and spongy brown fungi which gathered in piles like gigantic heaps of waste droppings from a beast who had spent the night in my front yard. And they were everywhere. Everywhere.

I snapped off a cap, discovering that the stem was attached to the side of the top, a most unusual arrangement. The underneath, like yellow ochre, was a maze-like network of wrinkles. This fungus had a name. *Gyrodon merulioides*. I hunted a long time to find that name, through three field guides, leafing past delicate mushrooms like earthstars, bird's nests, and inky caps. Even the flaming warnings on the *Amanita virosa*, destroying angel, did nothing to mar the beauty of that mushroom. But this grotesque fungus in my front yard was another story altogether.

After I identified *Gyrodon* and read about its love of ash trees, I resigned myself to its continued appearance for the next several weeks. The ash trees weren't going to go away and neither were the fungi who resided there.

But that didn't mean I had to like looking at them.

I have rearranged my chair in the front yard to face west, into the setting sun. But just behind me I can almost hear the fibrous underground network crawling closer to my back.

I will say one thing for the arrival of *Gyrodon*. I'm interested. My reading matter this week has been all about mushrooms, which seem just as foreboding to me as my *Gyrodon* looks, foreboding even by common name — but fascinating, too.

There is no question about the menacing nature of genus and species names like *Strobilomyces floccopus*, old man of the woods. It appears ancient and gnarled — and sounds contagious. In the field guide I find a chicken of the woods, too. I'd probably rather meet it at night than the old man. Would I like cauliflower fungus and earth tongues, pig's ear and chambered stinkhorn better than

Gyrodon? And what about several just made for Halloween — witches' butter, jack-o-lantern, and death cap, all with grotesque looking Latin names? I could scare myself silly just reading about fungi.

Maybe I'd be better off to read about bats, as the nights get darker and the frost coats the last awkward stalks of broccoli. If I turn my chair around again, and face east where the garden's corn hangs like discarded scarecrows, too quickly the night sky fills with bats. Those creatures have frightening Latin names too, like *Mormoops megalophylla*, Peter's ghost-faced bat.

Chills run up my spine. Unlike the mushrooms in my front yard, which I can examine for days on end and believe that I can beat into submission if the fungi decided to attack, the bats which fly over the pond and garden at night leave me no opportunity to identify them. They could be big brown bats or silver-haired bats or hoary bats or... My imagination swiftly runs away with me. Time to stop reading nonfiction. Edgar Allen Poe is next on my book pile.

A red ribbon
November, 1997

For a season of fanciful abandon, I'll take summer any day, but for a place of truth amidst gray contradiction, I'll pick November again and again. In this month nothing goes unnoticed. Every twig and branch of a tree, every dried stalk and frosted grass of the meadow, every granite outcropping and abandoned driftwood of the ocean are emphasized as the flames of October have finally consumed the last vestiges of the landscape's dress. Finally, everything has importance when the world appears bleak. To look at what is really around us is to look at ourselves clearly.

I thought about this idea a lot this weekend, with the rain slashing at us, ripping off the unfinished part of the barn roof so that hay and sheep are wet in one corner. Everything at the barn is gray and brown, unappealing. The paddock is filled with that suck-you-down kind of mud that makes swallowing noises when I put a foot anywhere inside the fence. It is a difficult time to tend to the animals and outdoor chores. Unlike the joys of spring, the months of green gardens, or the fury of autumn leaves, now I am left with the colors of this month seen in the grays of the barn.

It took something as simple as my chickens to remind me, however, that paradox exists now, the idea that we see clearly in the midst of murky darkness. Our black wild hen had chicks. She — as opposed to the more domesticated hens who stay in the coop at night — never settles anywhere, but with the help of the white wild hen, the two of them sitting like salt and pepper on the kitchen table brooding 13 eggs, they hatched 13 black baby chicks.

The chicks have refused to play by the rules, to stay put, now that they are two weeks old. A few inevitably huddle at night behind the sheep's watering trough. At Easter time I expect this. In November it is not easy. Perhaps that is the point — that none of this is easy.

Mother wild black hen collects most of the chicks, but there are always four or five who don't come in when called. The evening scene is always the same. It is late, cold, and dark, and I am searching along the edge of the barn sill, somewhere behind that trough in a spot that provides respite from the mud. My hand grabs something warm, hopefully not a rodent, and I pull out four chicks, tuck them into my pocket and deposit them in a sheep's manger where mama waits with the others. I slog back through the mud, feed Stanley, the black ram, and then finish haying the last of the sheep.

The bird feeders are no different, offering the same color fare, gray and black and white, with a little brown thrown in for good measure mixed among the mess of wet sunflower hulls. The chickadees are returning in great numbers, matched by the last of the fleeing slate-colored juncos. White-breasted and red-breasted nuthatches were prolific this summer and they, too, are frequenting the feeder. A few lonely sparrows add a dusting of brown. Even gold has changed to dust as goldfinches turn gray and begin to establish their winter routine. One solitary tufted titmouse has made our feeder home for three years, much to my delight, but he is not a sparkling color. No indeed. The feeder, too, is filled with November.

The story is the same down the road at Bess's place. All year long I deliver eggs on Saturday morning, guaranteeing a lively chat about green peas or yellow *helianthus* or pink roses. Now that November is here, I dash through the rain, snatching up last week's egg box from the porch steps, leaving the fresh eggs. Neighborliness with a heart is still there, but not covered with trappings. The color is gone.

Well — the color is not gone everywhere. There is one spot. In the middle of the paddock, west of the house, stands an old hemlock tree, November's symbol. Wrapped around its hefty trunk are three red ribbons. It is a bright spot. Red ribbons around the hemlock tree. I've designated this tree as the heart of November because of Pop. When he was ill the last Thanksgiving he came to visit, he watched that tree daily, calling it his "nearly perfect tree." He sat in his chair, looking at what was stripped bare and essential, and found contentment in the hours of the day, sometimes in the howling of wind and rain through branches dark and deserted, some days in shadows cast through hemlock branches by a muted setting sun, once when fog and clouds obscured the top of his tree. I have tied a red ribbon on this hemlock every November since Pop died.

It's what this month does to us. Rain and dark, skeletons of trees and houses and barns, dead grasses, bowed and broken. Then, suddenly out of the grayness, there appears a red ribbon. This Thanksgiving I will tie the fourth red ribbon on the hemlock tree. I do not know how many more it will wear, for that tree, too, is tired and dying. Some day a wild November windstorm will knock down something "nearly perfect," as is fitting. That is to be expected in November, a gray month with a warm heart.

Stan and Monty, two old men
December, 1997

Stan and Monty have entered into a gentlemen's agreement. On the surface it looks like Monty got the best end of the deal — the right to service the ewes, all 15 of them. In exchange Stan gets to be lord of the flock, in name only. For a year before this compromise, the arrangement had been hotly debated in our house as well as, I am sure, over grain in the manger. Stanley (he does have a rather formal name, although generally our farmers like to call him "Stan, my man") has been our stud ram for three years. That length of time is about adequate before inbreeding occurs.

We've had lambs, yearlings, and old ewes in love with him. Even our neighbor Susan is in love with Stan. With his thick black fleece, anyway. She uses it in elegant, artful creations that bear no resemblance whatsoever to the lumbering, 250 pound ram.

The time finally arrived when Stanley was no longer of use to the farm. Usually "no-use" spells muttonburger. But Stan's destiny altered. Hand-raised as a ram lamb, he remained tame and lovable in spite of a hormonal level which generally makes rams quite dangerous animals. Don't get me wrong. I never turned my back on Stan. But he didn't have the posture of, say, Oliver, another horned ram we once owned who, one evening, hit me so hard that my entire thigh was purple with bruises for a month.

With my husband and two sons rooting for Stan's continued sojourn with us, and at the same time acknowledging that we couldn't continue to house two full-grown rams, Pete loaded Stanley into the back of the dump truck and paid a visit to our trusty, big-animal veterinarian. He has been around a long time, and, without blinking an eye, he emasculated Stanley with a burdizzo. Stan was no longer Stan-the-man. He came back to the farm a bit dazed and exhausted, but content not to be mincemeat pies for the holidays.

Meanwhile, back at the ranch, Monty (whose formal name is Monticello) pranced around with his nose in the air. He is a thoroughbred Rambouillet from friends of ours, good solid farmers who came from the Midwest like we did years ago and are as surprised as we are to find ourselves still farming. Monty has graceful arching horns that wrap around his head like a coronet, giving him a king-like and disdainful air. He has a wide-eyed appearance, too, and I find myself trusting him as he continues to ignore me. Stan, on the other hand, has such black fleece and eyes that I can never tell where he is looking or guess what he is thinking, an especially disconcerting situation since his minor surgery. I wonder if he contemplates revenge. With Monty I am reassured that he is happy to be the stud and to pay me no heed.

We turned the 15 ewes loose with Monty and breeding began. In a month, after Stan was deemed safe, we turned him loose, too, now nothing but a has-been, a bellwether without the bell.

It all seems to be working out just fine. This holiday weekend, we marshaled the troops and all five of us spent two days in the barn cleaning up, building new pens, mucking out old ones, rebuilding a roof that had collapsed under the weight of last year's snow. Given the weather's track record so far this year, we felt a sense of urgency to get that repair solid. The kids hauled splintered wood away, built two new gates, and in general made the barn presentable.

While we labored, Stan hung around, waiting to have his ears scratched. He wagged his tail incessantly, rubbed his awkward old body against the hay baler, and nosed into everything we did.

Ignored for the moment, Monty led the ewes into the southwest pasture to frolic. But his harem days are numbered. By Sunday, Arek and I found ourselves in the shadowed west side of the barn with the sun setting, rapidly tying the last of the new gates into place. We were creating Monty's isolation pen. The ewes all appear pregnant now. They will need peace and quiet to chew their cuds, awaiting Christmas Eve and the coming birth of lambs in February and March. Monty gets to loiter in the corner — alone. Stan, however, is right in the thick of things, lying like the old man, ever the gentleman, lord of the flock, while the snowflakes of the newest storm turn him into a white sphinx.

The trees are still standing
January, 1998

Underlying the journeys I have taken in our woods and fields has been a search for grace in the seasons, in the events of the lives of the animals, family, and neighbors around me. That grace is a free gift, there for the taking — and surprisingly, too, for the giving. In the sharing of a sunset, in the divulging of secrets of the firefly, in the uncovering of spring's first violets — grace comes in the quiet, unexpected moment I give myself.

I am taking a close look around the farm this week, with quiet moments. The forest part of the farm has taken quite a beating from the recent ice storm. Along the west wall alone which separates our house from the paddock 40 ash trees have been damaged, their limbs mangled and torn at their base. True friends Jane and Phil came last Saturday to help cut and pile branches, mountains so high that many creatures will find shelter there, until the piles themselves become bonfires, an appeasement to the ice gods.

Initially, I shuddered when I looked at the damage to the trees. My husband was speechless. What were once graceful sentinels had become wounded creatures, ashamed of their appearance, with branches hanging like ragged clothing on a scarecrow. Once, a child of mine had said, "Them are trees. Them are truths." It didn't make much sense then, but perhaps it does now.

When the sun slips to the horizon, I am struck by the hurtful beauty that dazzles the eye. Weeks have passed and the ice has not gone. Stubborn and as resistant to change as we humans are, ice clings to the tiniest of bud ends and twigs. In the afternoon sunshine, those multiple surfaces blaze. Red, yellow, green blue, violet zing around the yard so rapidly I cannot count the prisms. My eyes no longer see the devastation but delight only in the wonder of crystallized trees. Indeed, there is truth there. We have weathered the storm, wounded in many places but not defeated. Grace remains in the beauty of birches weeping low beside white pines, frosted and mute. Sunshine will one day soon set them free to stand tall and spread their arms wide again, transformed but the same.

As if to affirm my hope for recovery, this afternoon seven redpolls slid across the ice-coated, open-platform bird feeder, readying themselves for avian Olympics and making me snatch my binoculars to revel in their pink breasts. Their arrival propels me ahead to maple sap running, mourning cloak butterflies emerging, and green grass growing again. I am eager for spring. Just thinking about it makes my old heart quicken, skip a beat now and then in anticipation.

Right now I am imagining the "new limbless look" to our farm. Certainly the garden will be opened up with much more summer sunlight available for the vegetables. If more insects infest the wounded trees, will there then be more bluebirds to eat the bugs? Maybe the raspberry crop will multiply. The house will be brighter — and hotter — but right now that sounds awfully nice.

Clearly, the gift of the seasons is one we need to cling to. In a technological, isolating world we need to be receivers of this grace, in the many seasons that have passed and in those to come — like lambing season which for us is right around the corner. This week I have been the keeper-of-sheep alone. I have kept my fingers crossed that lambs would not be born early while there was no one to help, and I have been lucky. Tonight I close the gate and call to Nell, who is barking in the distant wood at phantom sounds. Oh, there are real coyotes sometimes and the stirring of porcupines, but most likely these noises are just her imagination echoing off crystal trees.

She appears suddenly from the hemlocks. The trees cast strong shadows in the moonlight as we walk together back to the house. I know where grace is. It lies behind — and ahead. The trees are truths and they are still standing.

BOOK IV: TRUTHS

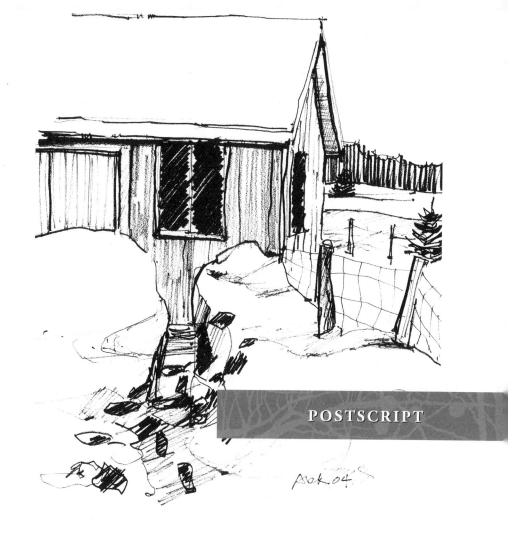

POSTSCRIPT

That which is seen
October, 2004

Last winter was exceptionally cold with little snow to ease the bone-chilling temperatures. My roses died in great numbers. Heathers, heaths, and lavender did not survive in spite of the precautions I took to cover them in the fall. Thyme did not grow. And Harlequin seemed to suffer worst of all.

Harlequin is not a plant but our oldest ewe. She has spent 14 winters with us, and, although we no longer breed her, we continue to value her contribution to the flock. Her demeanor is serene, a trait not common among the sheep, and this tranquility sometimes spreads to the others. With sixty sheep this past spring, we were grateful for a ewe who came to the barn when called and who distributed calmness throughout the flock.

In January when the temperatures continued to drop, we worried more and more about Harlequin. Fourteen is *old* age for a sheep (culling at age seven is not uncommon), and she was very thin in spite of worming medicine. She had no teeth, her fleece had not grown well, and we planned for her death.

But she lived on, showing no signs of pain or disability. By midwinter I decided that if Harlequin had a coat, a real one — not her scraggly fleece — to keep her warm, she might survive. Her indomitable spirit indicated she wasn't giving up this winter, so with a little help from Mid-States Wool Growers, I bought her a coat in a color called "medium sheep." I could have purchased red.

We put her new coat on at 7 a.m. Ten minutes later we opened the gate, Harlequin walked into the paddock, and five yearlings, 27 pregnant ewes, and Clover our cow all knocked down the paddock fencing, terrified by the intrusion of an apparition whose appearance was far from sheep-like.

The day passed, bitter cold and windy, with the 32 sheep and Clover standing *outside* the broken fence, staring into the paddock, where coated-Harlequin stood alone, slowly munching her way through the manger of hay. Without teeth it takes a long time to "gum" hay so she can swallow it, and that day, Harlequin had no competition for food. Gradually, the others came to accept her new look. Pete repaired the fence, and all went well for the entire winter.

Now that summer is over, Harlequin has actually fattened up, mainly because Pete feeds her at night with a small grain mixture. She comes to the south gate into the barn walkway and waits patiently until Pete lets her in. She walks immediately to her stall and spends the night there, returning to the flock at daybreak.

Why do we bother?

Feeding and caring for Harlequin is senseless in economic terms. But we have learned that there is more to this process than simply feeding ourselves. We love and carefully tend our animals. We make sure they get fresh air, sunshine, and green grass. As a family, we have worked hard to establish that thread within our life style which runs from sun to plants to animals to us.

Harlequin's stay with us is an example of our striving to commit to something other than just ourselves. Sometimes we don't succeed. Other times we do. The greatest value lies in knowing and caring for these animals. She was born on this farm, and it seems fitting that she should die on this farm when her time comes.

So, once again this fall, Harlequin's coat has been washed and is ready for her, should she need it.

Janet Galle • Two Farms

Epilogue

Like the changing seasons and the altered view through Jacob's art windows that hang from trees on our farm, our lives continue to evolve. Much to our delight, we have added a member to our family. Jillian married Aaron Wunsch with a reception at the farm in 2002. They live in Virginia. Both work in preserving old things, in the fields of archaeology and architectural history.

The land changes as well. Our west pasture is undergoing major renovation. Arek, who is a landscape architect, guides us as we expand the grass area, create a new pond, and push the forest back around the edges to keep coyotes at bay. We are studying the grass-fed beef movement, and I want to try growing a new bush, *Calycanthus floridus*, which my mother remembers from her childhood.

Since my last column at *The Times Record* many animals have come and gone from Apple Creek Farm. Huckleberry Pie died at age 19 and was buried near the garden she so loved. Parka, a spirited little black cat, joined us two years ago. Clover, a calf whose mother had no milk, came to us from Richard, another Bowdoinham farmer. We bottle fed her. She is exceptionally tame and, with none of her kind around, has learned to be the leader of the flock. The sheep love her. Perhaps foolishly — do we really want another cow? — we recently had her bred to a bull named New Frontier. (Artificial insemination is a wonderful thing.)

Nellie died this September. She had osteosarcoma, a bone cancer common to giant breeds. She learned to walk on three legs, continuing until the day she died to watch over the farm. "She was an inspiration," said Sue Chadima. When the end came, Sue put Nell to sleep while she sat upright, paws outstretched, waiting.